YORK NOTES

Metaphysical Poets

Note by Pamela M. King

Longman   York Press

Pamela M. King is hereby identified as author of this work in accordance with
Section 77 of the Copyright, Designs and Patents Act 1988

YORK PRESS
322 Old Brompton Road, London SW5 9JH

PEARSON EDUCATION LIMITED
Edinburgh Gate, Harlow,
Essex CM20 2JE, United Kingdom
Associated companies, branches and representatives throughout the world

First published 2001

ISBN 0–582–43158–1

Designed by Vicki Pacey
Phototypeset by Gem Graphics, Trenance, Mawgan Porth, Cornwall
Colour reproduction and film output by Spectrum Colour
Produced by Addison Wesley Longman China Limited, Hong Kong

CONTENTS

PART THREE

Critical Approaches

PART FOUR

Extended Commentaries

PART ONE

INTRODUCTION

HOW TO STUDY A POEM

Studying on your own requires self-discipline and a carefully thought-out work plan in order to be effective.

- Poetry is the most challenging kind of literary writing. In your first reading you may well not understand what the poem is about. Don't jump too swiftly to any conclusions about the poem's meaning.
- Read the poem many times, and including out loud. After the second or third reading, write down any features you find interesting or unusual.
- What is the poem's **tone** of voice? What is the poem's mood?
- Does the poem have an argument? Is it descriptive?
- Is the poet writing in his or her own voice? Might he or she be using a persona or mask?
- Is there anything special about the kind of language the poet has chosen? Which words stand out? Why?
- What elements are repeated? Consider alliteration, assonance, rhyme, rhythm, **metaphor** and ideas.
- What might the poem's **images** suggest or symbolise?
- What might be significant about the way the poem is arranged in lines? Is there a regular pattern of lines? Does the grammar coincide with the ending of the lines or does it 'run over'? What is the effect of this?
- Do not consider the poem in isolation. Can you compare and contrast the poem with any other work by the same poet or with any other poem that deals with the same **theme**?
- What do you think the poem is about?
- Every argument you make about the poem must be backed up with details and quotations that explore its language and organisation.
- Always express your ideas in your own words.

This York Note offers an introduction to metaphysical poetry and cannot substitute for close reading of the text and the study of secondary sources.

New writing often emerges from cultures which are going through rapid change or trauma. The first half of the seventeenth century in England, when the so-called metaphysical poets wrote, provided both. On one hand there was the excitement of new scientific discoveries which could not help but affect the way people saw themselves in relation to one another, to the world, the universe and God. Galileo's telescope had demonstrated once and for all that the scandalous notion put forward by Copernicus years before – that the earth was not the centre of the universe – was unavoidably true. At the same time, the known world was growing. The American continent had been discovered over a hundred years earlier, but this was the period of mapping and settlement, of discovering just how big and how rich in resources it was.

On the other hand deep rifts developed at home. The Church was bitterly divided into increasingly extreme factions from Roman Catholicism to Puritanism. The royal court, first under James I, then Charles I, steadily withdrew into its own lavish cocoon, causing political unrest amongst the gentry from the shires who made up a Parliament which was rarely called, so could not rule. The outcome was a period of violence and civil strife which divided families and tore the country apart. Whether you choose to call it the Great Rebellion, the Civil Wars, the English Revolution or, in the despairing words of a contemporary general, simply 'this war without an enemy' (see Ollard, 1976), the events of the mid century brought changes in British culture so extreme that, despite the Restoration of the monarchy, there was no going back to the old power structures ever again.

The category 'metaphysical poetry' causes problems for the modern reader, for it depends on certain questionable assumptions about what poetry does, what it is for and how we read it. In the study of English literature, everyone understands that it refers to the work of John Donne, George Herbert, Henry Vaughan, Andrew Marvell and a number of optional extras. Their poems, by and large, are short, draw their subject matter from the major preoccupations of their age, and are characterised by an impatience with conventional forms of expression and the adoption of startling innovations, particularly in their handling of **imagery** The device known as the metaphysical **conceit**, which makes improbable comparisons, epitomises the verbal wittiness which these poets seem to have in common.

Y

But these poets shared no overt literary manifesto (unlike, for example, Wordsworth and Coleridge at a later date); they wrote on widely divergent subjects, from widely divergent points of view. Some of them did know one another, but as a group their differing cultural and ideological circumstances are undeniable. Carew was a young courtier in the immediate circle surrounding Charles I, Richard Crashaw a Roman Catholic exile, Andrew Marvell tutor to the daughter of a great Parliamentarian general. Metaphysical poetry is a category imposed by literary critics which has stuck. It depends on a view of poetry that tends to ignore the context or process of its production in favour of viewing poetry as some kind of higher form of expression which exists apart and is accessible to anyone who can decipher its codes down the ages. It now seems increasingly strained to categorise poets by technicalities of their writing, when the major thrust of present-day literary criticism is to place writing in its culture, particularly when the poetry in question also offers a range of insistent cultural and political statements. In reading this poetry, then, the modern reader needs to attend to the differences between these poets as much as their similarities. The term 'metaphysical poetry' is there to be understood, but then to be questioned. It survives as a flag of convenience, permitting modern editors to continue to publish anthologies of some exciting and intense individual poems from a politically and ideologically turbulent period in the history of Britain.

PART TWO

COMMENTARIES

The majority of the poems commented on in this section are drawn from *A Selection of Metaphysical Poets*, a Heinemann Poetry Bookshelf anthology edited by Virginia Graham (1996). Not all the poems in this anthology are individually summarised, but cross references are made to those not covered in detail, so that common themes and techniques can be identified. Many of these poems are densely packed and challenging, as many of their ideas and modes of expression will be new to the modern reader: efforts have been made to select the trickiest, and in many cases the most famous, for quite detailed textual analysis. Three poems in the anthology not dealt with in this section are printed in full and given still more detailed attention in Extended Commentaries, where they are joined by two poems not in the anthology but considered of central interest to the study of metaphysical poetry.

An introduction to each of the poets featured, along with some general remarks about the nature of their poetic output, is available in the Background section The Poets. Single editions of their work are listed in Further Reading. The standard anthology remains *The Metaphysical Poets*, edited by Helen Gardner (Penguin Books, 1957), while David Norbrook and H.R. Woudhuysen's *The Penguin Book of Renaissance Verse 1509–1659* (1992) sets these poets in their wider contemporary context. Poems referred to in this Note which are not printed in *A Selection of Metaphyiscal Poets* can all be found in this latter anthology or in *The New Oxford Book of English Verse*, edited by Helen Gardner (1972). All biblical quotations in this Note are taken from the King James, or Authorised, Version of the Bible, a translation contemporary with the poems being studied.

JOHN DONNE

John Donne wrote erotic poetry, poetry about mutual love and religious poetry, all of which are represented here. It is dangerous to see these three categories as representing different phases in his own life; he seems to have written from all three points of view at a variety of times.

E LEGY: TO HIS MISTRESS GOING TO BED

Undress for me, and I shall undress for you

Hurry up and undress for bed while I am still aroused. I am not one of those who are distracted by your layers of gorgeous clothing – indeed, I envy the garment that is closer to your body than I am. Allow my hands to wander over your body like an explorer in uncharted territory full of undiscovered riches. I am overjoyed by your nakedness; a book is better than its cover. And since you generously allow me to see all of you, look, I am naked before you also.

> Donne manipulates the conventional device of **Renaissance** love poetry, the **blazon** (see Love), and instead of listing his lover's physical attributes, lists the garments he wants her to remove. The poem develops an overall sense of dramatic sexual urgency by its use of the **imperative mood**. Throughout, the woman is portrayed as territory, the man as the imperial invading force, however benign, and the repetition of 'my' asserts his ownership. The **imagery** which the poet uses to construct the contrasting gender roles of the man and the woman draws fashionably on classical mythology, but is also topical, referring directly to recent discoveries in astronomy and particularly in geography. The woman is addressed not only as 'America' but as a 'new found land' (line 27). Newfoundland on the eastern seaboard of Canada had very recently been discovered. The temporary nature of the male lover's sexual arousal is twice described obliquely. First it is compared to the soldier who, ready for battle, begins to lose the power to withstand the enemy if he is kept standing too long without action. Second the effect of the lover stripped down to her white undergarment is contrasted with a ghost: the sight of a ghost makes hair stand on end, whereas she makes his flesh stand erect. Typically metaphysical, the poem at once evokes an intimate dramatic moment – bedtime for two lovers – while the choice of imagery proposes that events have vast universal significance.

5 **heaven's zone** the stars forming the belt on the figure seen to be represented in the constellation of Orion

11 **busk** boned bodice, corset

16 **diadem** wire framework, coronet

23 **sprite** ghost, spirit

29 **empery** empire

31 **bonds** confining ropes or chains

36 **Atlanta's** mythological Greek female runner, who married Hippomenes because he defeated her in a race by dropping golden apples which she stopped to pick up

42 **imputed** alleged

THE FLEA   What more is loss of virginity than a flea bite?

Look at this flea which has bitten us both and note that the loss of your virginity to me would be no worse than this. No, don't kill it; it bears three lives in one and, containing both our bloods, is our marriage bed. Oh, you have. How cruel! What had it done except take a drop of blood? The amount of honour you will lose in succumbing to me is as trivial as the threat to your life from this flea bite.

The poem is built around **juxtapositions**. The principal one is the contrast between the microscopic flea and the bodies of the two lovers. Contrast in size is extended into contrast in importance, as a couple of flea bites are equated with the mingling of bodily fluids in sex. The woman's casual gesture in killing the flea with her fingernail is then contrasted with the extreme moral scruples that are apparently causing her to postpone losing her virginity.

As in many of Donne's love poems, he uses poetic comparisons to open up weightier underlying considerations about the nature of physical existence, the world's mutability and the status of the individual in relation to the universe. He also deploys religious vocabulary which gives an edge to the poem as its **metaphors** verge on the blasphemous. In this poem the object of attention is subjected to microscopic attention beyond what is visible to the naked eye, reminding the reader that the poem was written in an era when the telescope not only opened up the universe and an understanding of humanity's place within it, but enabled the viewer to manipulate the size of any object of attention at will. The flea actually, as well as figuratively, changes size, and its gorging with blood has evident sexual **connotations**. The mingling of three bloods within its 'walls of jet' (line 15) is an **image** of containment, suggesting that the lovers' space is the only essential reality. Time too is slowed right down so that the moment of watching the flea move, bite and savour, then move on, is elevated to a moment of infinite leisure and intimacy for the two lovers. Nonetheless, the male voice in the poem is assertive, seeking to impose rational scientific observation over the female's action and her withholding of sexual favours, which are presented as intuitive and are, by implication, therefore devalued.

6 **maidenhead** virginity

10 **stay** stop

15 **cloistered** contained as in a monastery

16 **apt** appropriate

18 **sacrilege** crime against God, i.e. murder and suicide

THE GOOD MORROW

We are each completed by being together

We weren't alive until we loved each other. In being together we create our own entire world. Two benign hemispheres are contained in the reflection of each lover in the other's eye, this world having no cold polar region, no dark night. Death is a product of imbalance; the perfect equilibrium of our love for each other is immortal.

This is another of Donne's love poems characterised by the creation of an emphatic voice, questioning and exclaiming at the worth of life without love. The speaker insists that lovers have no interest in anything outside of each other, an idea which he develops to suggest that outside the relationship nothing is real. This initial proposal is then supported by a typical **conceit** which compares the reflection of the face of each lover in the other's eye with the two hemispheres which go to make up the world. The larger world is still being explored and mapped, is known to contain the inhospitable northern regions, and goes dark when the sun sets in the west at night. The further conceit that love transcends mortality is proposed in the final lines, drawing on Galen's classical theories of medicine whereby disease and death are caused by an imbalance of the bodily humours; the eternal has perfect equilibrium such as he finds in the mutuality of their love.

Like many of Donne's other love poems, here the voice of the lover acknowledges the excitement of geographical and scientific discovery, as well as the heritage of ancient learning, only to dismiss it. He also invokes the **paradox** of love as both a liberator and a force which has the power to entrap and confine its willing victims in time and space, as each becomes bound by an equal and opposite other.

1 **by my troth** verbal tag, with little meaning, but giving the sense of a speaking voice

3 **country pleasures** aristocratic children were sent into the country to be wet-nursed; 'country' also implies sexual, in a debased animalistic sense

4 **snorted** snored

4 **seven sleepers' den** seven legendary young Christians were persecuted by Decius (AD249), but they survived being walled up alive by sleeping for 187 years

5 **fancies** products of the imagination

13 **maps ... worlds on worlds** charts of the heavens

17 **hemispheres** half spheres (of the globe)

See also 'The Anniversary', which observes that although everything material ages from year to year, love cannot decay but transcends the laws of time and change, and 'A Valediction: of Weeping', in which it is argued that if a map-maker can draw the continents upon a ball, the parting lovers' tears and sighs can become a whole stormy ocean in which to drown.

SONG (GO, AND CATCH A FALLING STAR)

Beautiful woman cannot be faithful

Go and perform impossible tasks; go on an impossibly long journey and see incredible sights; but I still defy you to find a beautiful woman who will be faithful to her lover. If you do find one, tell me so that I can go to meet her. On second thoughts, don't bother, because she too will have been unfaithful before I can count to three.

The whole song is built around the impossibility **topos**, proposing that it is easier to catch a falling star, for example, than to find a woman who is both beautiful and faithful. The poem is **metrically** complex, based on a nine-line stanza, with the seventh and eighth lines set as a rhyming **couplet** with only two syllables per line. It lends itself to musical setting, particularly the beat-counting device of the final line, and has been set to music a number of times in the centuries since it was written. The insistent and indignant voice of the disappointed lover, who changes his mind in the middle of the final stanza, is characteristic of a **courtly love lyric**. This time the poem is addressed, presumably, to another man, in a supposed dramatic setting where the action will be completed by his writing a letter answering the challenge posed by the speaker. The impossibility topos is more reminiscent of traditional fairy tales and folk songs, for example 'Are You Going to Scarborough Fair?'

2 **mandrake** a plant with a forked root, supposed to resemble a man's legs and genitals, and often said to have aphrodisiac properties
4 **cleft** cut in two (the devil reputedly has cloven hooves)

See also 'The Undertaking', which proposes precisely the opposite: virtue can lie within beauty, but, if you find it, it is best to keep the fact secret! 'Song (Sweetest love, I do not go)' is a lyric which is also metrically complicated, changing rhythm midway through each stanza and thereby achieving a kind of **syncopation**. Carew's 'A Song' also uses the impossibility topos.

THE SUN RISING

Dawn disturbs lovers

Interfering sun, you should leave lovers alone in the morning and instead bother people who need to get up. You are not so powerful: I could shut you off by closing my eyes, except that I don't want to take my eyes off my lover. If you can still see after looking at her, tell me tomorrow if anything you pass today is as beautiful as she is. She is all places, I am all rulers, we are everything; so if you want to rest, stay and warm us here, as this room is the whole world.

The conceit (see The Metaphysical Conceit) in this poem is a familiar one in Donne's love poetry, building on the proposal, as in 'The Good Morrow', that lovers are the whole world to each other, a reversal of large and small. To serve his central theme that lovers are the centre of the universe, Donne here wittily ignores Copernican astronomy (see Ideas & Discoveries) and reverts to the older belief that the sun moves round the earth. The sun is **personified** and addressed as an interfering old busybody who cannot distinguish between schoolboys, huntsmen, apprentices and agricultural labourers, all of whom need to get up early, and lovers who want to lie all day in bed. The second stanza further reduces the size and importance of the sun in relation to the lovers by suggesting that it can be switched off by the closing of eyes. Similarly, in the third stanza the speaker suggests that only the lovers have absolute centrality and quintessential substance, and that all earthly power and riches merely imitate them. The sun's imagined orbit of the earth provides an opportunity to mention dismissively the exotic New World riches of the East and West Indies. The relationship between the man and the woman is not an equal one. The woman is characterised as territory which can be mapped and mined, the man as ruler, map-maker and, by extension, imperial exploiter of the woman's mercantile potential. The poem ends with the suggestion that love can countermand the laws of science and nature, thereby completing the verbal exercise in manipulating both time and space.

7 **court-huntsmen** servants who arranged hunting expeditions for the royal court
8 **country ants** agricultural labourers
9 **clime** climate
14 **lose her sight** lose sight of her
17 **both th'Indias** the East Indies, exploited for spices, and the West Indies, for gold
23 **play** imitate, as in the theatre
24 **mimic** imitation
24 **alchemy** the bogus science which attempted to turn base metal to gold
30 **sphere** according to the discarded model of the universe which Donne is wittily invoking here, each heavenly body was contained within its own transparent crystalline sphere

See also 'Elegy: To his Mistress Going to Bed' for the unequal nature of the relationship between the sexes: the man as conqueror, the woman as territory. Like 'The Good Morrow', the poem invokes and negates science, learning and historical progress to manoeuvre the speaker into a point of paralysis, such that the power to release him lies in the reader's willingness to accept the arguments. Andrew Marvell's 'To his Coy Mistress' also suggests that love is above the laws of science and nature.

THE CANONIZATION

Life is not worth living without love

Do what you want, say what you will about me, so long as you will let me love. Don't tell me I am too old for this; you go and seek fame or wealth, if that is what matters to you, and leave me alone. What is damaged, what changed, by my love for her? Whatever we are, we are made by loving each other; this love completes us. If we cannot live in this love, let us die in it, and if we are unfit for a tomb, let love poems be our memorial. All lovers take example from us in knowing that love epitomises all that is essential in existence.

In the first two stanzas the person who is the object of love is not discussed; it is only in the third stanza that the **first person** becomes plural and, at the same time, the poem moves into a series of ingenious **metaphors** with strong sexual **connotations**. In the fourth stanza the poem then turns in on itself, asserting that if no other monument is judged fit for this unapproved love, it will be commemorated in verse. **Sonnets** and hymns are **juxtaposed** with historical chronicle as fitting memorial, and those short verse forms are in turn compared with the 'well wrought urn' (line 33) as being more fit for holding the ashes of the deceased than 'half-acre tombs' (line 34). Here Donne uses the language of religion to describe human passion, and the verses become hymns which will lead to the lovers becoming saints.

The final stanza draws on Neoplatonic philosophy (see Platonic Philosophy) in pushing the argument further and asserting that the eyes of the lovers hold together the quintessence of everything in the world, which then must look to them for its perfect pattern. The poem's argument is, ultimately, a rejection of Neoplatonism as it is also a refusal to accept that there can be any pure universal essence beyond the sensory world. The initial projection of a lover whose love has met opposition, along with **allusions** to the material ruin brought about by love, has caused many critics to impose an autobiographical reading on the poem, although an understanding of its central argument depends more on broader cultural understandings than on the retrievable events of the poet's life.

Canonization creation of saints, often following their martyrdom; here implied as the outcome of ruination brought about by illicit love

2 **chide my palsy** cite the signs of ageing in me (as reasons for knowing better than to ruin my life for love)

7 **real, or his stamped face** the king's actual face or his face on coins (i.e. seek prestige at court, or material wealth)

13 **forward** early

15 **plaguy bill** list of those dead of the plague

17 **Litigious** keen to use the law to solve grievances

20 **fly** moth or butterfly

21 **tapers** candles

22 **the eagle and the dove** strength and gentleness; the male and the female

23 **phoenix** unique mythical bird said to renew itself by burning

31 **chronicle** historical narrative

33 **urn** vessel for the ashes of the dead

38 **hermitage** place for solitary religious retreat

40–1 **extract ... glasses** refers to alchemical experiment, where quintessential matter is produced in glass vessels

See also 'The Prohibition', which debates the extremes of love. The lover who loves him too much is in danger of being destroyed by his death, whereas, if she hates him, she may kill him. If he is to live, she must both love and hate him simultaneously. 'The Expiration' proposes a direct correlation between loss of love and death.

AIR AND ANGELS

We can find equilibrium in our love

Before I met you I already loved you in essence, so when I met you I could not actually see you, for I was dazzled. Just as my soul had to take on a body to live, so too did love, which is the soul's child, and the body love took on was you. I thought giving love bodily form would help me proceed, but even one of your hairs overburdens me. Love cannot survive in nothing, but nor can it survive in too much, nor in brilliant fragmentation. Only together will our loves find stability like a sphere containing a heavenly body. Your love must be the embodiment of my love, as an angel's body is fashioned out of formless air.

The poem's argument depends on an understanding of a number of metaphysical theories inherited by Donne's age. The first stanza reflects the Neoplatonic argument (see Platonic Philosophy) that the loved one's body is incidental, because what the lover really perceives is the reflection in an individual of pure divine love. The beginning of the second stanza suggests, using a **metaphor** taken from shipping, that love is steadied by having a physical object on which to fix. But this woman is so overwhelmingly beautiful that instead of being steadied by meeting her, the speaker is in danger of being toppled over. The stanza then further complicates the argument by drawing on the science of metaphysics itself, which argues that next to spirit, air is the purest of elements, and that angels are made all of air, congealed by the will of God so that they can appear to human beings. The uniting of their two loves – one air, the other angel – forms the stable sphere in which his love can operate as an effective intelligence, in the same way as planetary bodies were believed to revolve in an orderly manner because each was fixed within a transparent sphere. The poem is difficult to interpret not only because it refers to specific scientific beliefs, but also because its **syntax** is complex, mimicking a scholastic proof. Its **theme** concerns the transcendent nature of mutual love, which is an eternal, stable, spiritual essence far beyond the simple uniting of two material beings.

15 **ballast** stabilise (a ship) by putting weights in the bottom

18 **pinnace** lightweight sailing boat

18 **overfraught** too heavily laden

See also 'The Canonization' and 'The Anniversary', both of which use different fields of **imagery** to assert the balance and durability of mutual love.

A VALEDICTION: FORBIDDING MOURNING

Lovers, though apart, cannot be separated

Let us part without fuss, in the manner of virtuous men on their deathbeds. All movement in the universe causes anxiety but is benign. Inferior earthbound lovers cannot stand to be parted, but we are so much one mind and soul that we care less about physical proximity. Indeed, as we are one, we become larger the farther apart we are. We are like a pair of compasses, where you are the fixed centre point and I the other point that moves around but always returns to that to which it is joined.

Donne draws heavily upon scientific **imagery** in this poem about lovers parting. The proposition is common in his love poetry that the two lovers are refined by love into one single essence. Drawing on the traditional image of the universe with earth at its centre, he compares his relationship favourably with those who live below the moon, on earth. They are dependent on proximity to maintain their love, and are discomfited by any movement in the heavens. The superior nature of his love is then defined through two memorable **conceits**. Firstly he alleges that since the two lovers are one single substance, when they are apart their love is expanded, not diminished, like gold beaten out into gold leaf. He then compares his departure, leaving his lover behind, to the movement of a pair of compasses: his lover is the fixed foot and he the moving one. As he moves farther off she leans towards him, and as he comes home to her he grows erect. The conceit, despite the poem's earlier denial of the physical, has clear sexual meaning.

Compasses were an instrument much used in the contemporary project of map-making, and here again Donne pictures the lovers as on a map: the woman being a fixed place, the man exploring at will. The conceit was borrowed by the poet Katherine Philips in

'Friendship in Embleme, or the Seal. To my dearest Lucasia', a poem addressed to a female friend from whom she was enduring an enforced parting. Philips, however, subtly changes the comparison, so that where Donne's version implies a hierarchy in the relationship, hers is an image of absolute mutuality in love:

The Compasses that stand above
Express this great immortal Love;
For Friends, like them, can prove this true,
They are, and yet they are not, two.

And in their posture is exprest
Friendship's exalted Interest:
Each follows where the other leans,
And what each does, this other means. (lines 21–8)

Valediction leave-taking
1 **pass mildly away** die quietly
7 **profanation** blasphemy
8 **laity** uninitiated (usually in the religious sense; here love is the religion)
11 **trepidation** trembling
13 **sublunary** below the moon (i.e. on earth)
16 **elemented** created its substance
17 **refined** made pure
31 **hearkens** pays attention
34 **obliquely** at an angle
35 **just** exact

See also 'Song (Sweetest love, I do not go)', which engages in some **sophistry** on the same theme, suggesting that, as the two are one, they cannot truly be parted, and, because they are one, the more she weeps and worries about him, the more likely it is that ill will befall him. That being the case, her lamenting is 'unkindly kind' (line 27), an **oxymoron** relying on two possible meanings of 'unkindly': 'cruelly' but also 'unnaturally'. In 'Elegy: On his Mistress' the speaker considers the pros and cons of taking his lover overseas with him and, on deciding she should not come, prays they will both live until he returns. In 'A Valediction: of Weeping' the poet builds a whole argument around the metaphysical conceit (see The Metaphysical

Conceit) that tears will form an ocean to drown in, made stormy by sighs, so grief at parting threatens safe return.

THE RELIC   Unconsummated love lasts for ever

When my grave is opened for another burial and the grave-digger finds a circle of fair hair around the bone, will he realise it is a lover's grave and leave it alone? If this happens in a superstitious land, will they take our remains back with them and worship us in their churches, believing that, like the saints worshipped in the old faith, we can perform miracles? Ours was a pure love, no more concerned with sex than the angels are; we never touched sexually or gave way to the natural instincts which marriage makes respectable. But now I cannot find words to express what a miracle she was.

The power of the poem is that it appears intensely personal and written out of a specific, highly emotional situation without the reader being sufficiently informed about what that situation is. It is a poem about mutual love, but love that is unconsummated, possibly because one or both parties are married. Its central **image** depends on the biblical promise that on the Day of Judgement everyone who has ever lived will be resurrected body and soul: if one lover wears round the wrist a lock of the other's hair they are bound to be united in eternity, as people scurry around collecting their bodies. Mary Magdalen was the prostitute who became a follower of Jesus and was the first to meet him after the Resurrection, but here she is used simply as an example of a beautiful, sexually experienced saint, with whom the woman here is compared, in another unconsummated love relationship. The idea of keeping relics of the dead refers back to the Roman Catholic practice of preserving the bones of saints, believing that they have miraculous powers of healing. Here the 'mis-devotion' (line 13) refers to those who may foolishly worship the bones of the lovers instead of love itself. The only miracle these lovers have performed is the intimate one of having preserved a perfect, chaste love.

Commentators used to claim that the poem was addressed to Magdalen Herbert, George Herbert's mother. A celebrated society beauty, she was seven years older than Donne, and was his friend when he was a young father. There is, however, no evidence – and no need – to believe that she is the subject of the poem in order to read it adequately, as much of its emotional power depends upon its indeterminacy.

2 **guest** here a corpse, because of the common practice of the time to reuse old graves

3 **woman-head** not a virgin, i.e. a bed used before

13 **mis-devotion** wrongful worship, idolatry, superstition

21 **paper** the piece of paper on which this poem is written

26 **angels** angels are sexless

29 **seals** prohibitions on natural sexual love set by law

30 **late law** marriage, a law imposed by civilisation on the earlier natural state of humanity

32 **pass** surpass

See also 'The Funeral', which refers to exactly the same subject but at an earlier imagined point in time, when the speaker is being laid out for burial and the same circle of hair is found on his arm. Here he sees the lover's hair as offering a better chance of preserving him intact beyond the grave than she ever did in life, when by refusing to consummate their love she refused to make him whole. A more pessimistic image of unfulfilled love is presented in 'Twickenham Garden', also attributed to the effect on the poet of loving a lady who was unattainable because she was married. There, far from having a transcendent effect, his 'spider love' (line 6) taints everything around him, like a reversal of the transformation achieved with wine and bread at mass.

*H*OLY SONNETS

Throughout his life, John Donne wrote Petrarchan **sonnets** (see Sonnet) debating religious themes from a highly personal point of view. The speaker is preoccupied with the possibility that he might not achieve salvation but instead might go to hell, not because of sins committed, but because Calvinist beliefs, which were gaining influence when Donne wrote, suggested that everyone was predestined for either heaven or hell, and that the capacity for sin or virtue was simply symptomatic of a predestined fate (see Religion & the Church).

AT THE ROUND EARTH'S IMAGINED CORNERS

This sonnet is set at the moment of the Last Judgement. The **octave** repeats in detail the events predicted in Matthew 25 and pictured in numerous paintings. Those to be resurrected will include all who drowned in Noah's flood and those who are alive on the last day, who will not have to die at all. In the **sestet** the speaker returns to the present, musing that Doomsday will be too late to repent, so he had better do so now, cleansing himself of his sins as thoroughly as if he had a legal document pardoning him, signed with Christ's blood.

BATTER MY HEART, THREE-PERSONED GOD

This sonnet launches a powerful challenge to God in Trinity (Father, Son and Holy Ghost) to use force to knock down what the speaker has been and renew him as a better man. The second **quatrain** uses a **simile** comparing the speaker to a conquered city in the power of an alien invader, presumably the devil. He would let God in, but is too weak to repel the adversary. Reason, the quality inherited from God which distinguishes humanity from the animals, is God's deputy within, but has proved in this case too weak. In the sestet the **image** changes to one of marriage. However dearly the speaker loves God, he is betrothed to the devil. He pleads with God to divorce him from that betrothal. The sonnet's final **couplet** depends on two **paradoxes**: only by being imprisoned by God can the speaker be free; then, with an audacious shift into sexual imagery, only by being spiritually raped by God can he be truly pure.

SINCE SHE WHOM I LOVED HATH PAID HER LAST DEBT

This was written on the death of Donne's wife. The speaker reflects that the death of a loved one has benefited both her, as she is in heaven, and him, as it has focused him keenly on a yearning for God. As people are provoked by running water to seek out its source, he has an insatiable spiritual thirst for God (one of the symptoms of dropsy is thirst). In the sestet the speaker corrects himself by considering that God's love is already available to him, offered as a replacement for his wife's. It is God who fears losing his love, not only to saints and angels, trappings of the Roman Catholic faith which Donne left behind, but to the temptations of the seven deadly sins, expressed again in the tripartite scheme as the sins of the world (anger and envy), the flesh (gluttony, sloth and lechery) and the devil (pride and avarice). This poem bears comparison with John Milton's sonnet beginning 'Methought I saw my late espoused Saint', also written on the death of his wife.

GOOD FRIDAY, 1613. RIDING WESTWARD

Worldly concerns conflict with worshipping God

Assume man's soul is one of the heavenly spheres, moved by devotion to God and, being affected by external forces, unable to control itself fully; so while it wants to move east, in the direction of God, it is impelled west. Yet I am almost glad not to have to watch the Crucifixion; it would be too much to watch God die, a sight which caused an earthquake and eclipse, or even to look at the Virgin Mary mourning at the base of the Cross. As I ride westward, however, that sight remains in my memory, and I know you are watching me. As you hang on the Cross I turn my back on you, but only so that you can whip me. Punish me until you can recognise in me a better image of yourself, and then I'll turn to face you.

Good Friday is the anniversary of the Crucifixion, but the speaker is, **figurally**, riding away from the scene, conventionally pictured in the east, the location of heaven and the rising sun, always a potential **pun** on God's son, Christ. The west is not the location of hell, conventionally in the north, but of the world. Hence the poem is an expression of the speaker's distraction by concerns of the world. He carries wherever he goes an image in his memory of the Crucifixion anyway. The **conceit** he uses to explain these contrary impulses depends upon an understanding of the theory of the universe which placed the earth at the centre, a theory finally disputed by scientists of Donne's own day but still prevalent in literature. The speaker is like one of the planets contained in its crystal sphere, impelled in one direction by the 'first mover' (line 8), the engine of the system, while its own impulse is to move in the opposite direction, an effort which means it takes a year to accomplish a single orbit. As he resolutely rides westward, he considers that he is glad not to have to face up to the agony of the Crucifixion, a sight reputed to have induced an earthquake and eclipse of the sun. Yet the reader is treated to a detailed description of the sight because it is what the speaker carries in his memory, the details drawing on conventional meditations on the Passion where systematic concentration on detail was intended to provoke penance.

At the end the speaker suggests that God should take the opportunity of his turned back to scourge him, so that he can be purified by punishment. The whole poem is characterised by questioning, suggesting the speaker's uncertainty of his own spiritual strength and resolve. Its opening statement reads more like an algebraic problem in which the reader is required to accept certain equivalences for the sake of argument.

2 **intelligence** according to Platonic philosophy, the planets were sentient beings

12 **endless day beget** when Christ's sun/son set, it abolished the 'night' of death and damnation

19 **lieutenant Nature** the personification of the forces which govern the things of the earth is conventionally presented as God's deputy in the business of creation

20 **footstool** Isaiah 66:1 describes the world as God's footstool, and Matthew 27:51 reports that there was an earthquake at the moment of Christ's death on the Cross

21 **span the poles** Christ's body stretched on the Cross is conventionally pictured as overshadowing the four corners of the earth

22 **tune all spheres** the universe made up of crystalline spheres was believed to play celestial music as it turned

24 **Zenith ... antipodes** the Cross stretches above us as high as the eye can see and below to the bottom of the world

28 **apparel** clothing, i.e. God in becoming man put on the flesh as his clothing

31 **furnished** provided, i.e. the Virgin Mary, as Christ's mother, provided him with bodily form, while God provided his spirit

32 **ransomed** bought off, i.e. the sacrifice of the Crucifixion repaid Adam's original sin in which all humanity participates and which allowed the devil to imprison humankind

40 **rusts** tarnishings of sin

See also the **sonnets** 'Oh, to vex me', in which the speaker complains of his contrary impulses, and 'Batter my heart, three-personed God', in which he pleads for God's purifying punishment. The poem also has much in common with George Herbert's poems of internal conflict, for example 'Jordan (I)', 'Jordan (II)', 'The Pulley' and 'The Collar'. Many of the themes of this poem, echoed in the *Holy Sonnets*, are simply resolved in 'A Hymn to God the Father', which sees fear itself as a sin, a lack of faith in the power of God's forgiveness through the Crucifixion; focusing on that is the only remedy for fear.

GEORGE HERBERT

The poems studied here, like all Herbert's surviving poems, deal with a single theme, which is the human being's relationship with God, through a number of ingenious comparisons and images.

THE CHURCH-FLOOR

Church buildings embody the faith

The tiles on the church floor stand for virtues – the speckled ones for patience, the black ones for humility. The change in the level of the floor towards the choir is confidence, and the cement that binds the whole together is love. Sin stains the marble, but marble weeps, which removes sin. Death sometimes blows dust around, but actually sweeps it. God is the architect who gives such strength to the weak.

The poem is very preacherly. It is part of the devotional collection called *The Temple* in which Herbert uses **typology** to turn the plain and simple concrete features of an Anglican church building into an explanation of the Christian faith. The church in question has been associated with King's College Chapel in Cambridge, a building of apparent simplicity of line but rich in meaningful detail. Here elements of the church floor become virtues, the tiles patience and humility, fitting for something walked upon. The floor, however, changes level as it moves into the choir. Architecturally the choir describes that part of a church building at the east end, where the altar is and where the officiating clergy are situated during worship. The choir is **symbolically** nearer to God, and tends to be elevated, so is fittingly compared to the reward for patience and humility, which is confidence in God, and therefore in personal salvation as promised in the sacrament of the altar. The cement which glues the entire floor together is love, or charity (Latin *caritas* translates as love), the reciprocal altruistic bond between Christ and the believer.

The **allegory** is then extended to demonstrate how the properties of the floor as described in the first stanza fit it to guard against attack. The accumulation of dirt in the veins of the marble is equated with sin, which is 'cleansèd when the marble weeps' (line 15). It is a natural property of marble to sweat, or to accumulate condensed moisture on its surface in damp climates. Death, the wind blowing through the door, attempts to distribute dust, but ends up sweeping it. It is a tenet of Christianity that God often tricks malign forces into doing good inadvertently. The architect of this church floor is, of course, God, celebrated for designing so many fortifications for humanity's natural weakness.

13 **steals** sneaks in

14 **curious veins** intricate pattern on marble which looks like veins

See also 'The Windows', where Herbert uses another element in the fabric of the church as a **metaphor** for and in contrast to the priest. The priest is an imperfect window on God's truth, but his efforts are assisted by the stories fixed in the stained glass windows.

JORDAN (I)   **How to write about God**

Who says that poetry has to be contrived to be good? Must everything be expressed obscurely? Can poetry be written only about fantasy landscapes and their unreal inhabitants? I do not want to write about that, nor will I accept criticism of poems which (unlike this one) worship God directly.

The poem is anti-poetry. It is critical of the contrived nature of contemporary secular poetry and, in particular, the **pastoral** conventions of love poetry. The poem invokes Plato's view that earthly things are poor reflections of the divine, so the representation of earthly things in art is doubly removed from God. The **image** of the shepherd sharply focuses the tension between secular and devotional poetry; the idealised shepherds in classical pastoral –

Y

imitated in, for example, Shakespeare's *As You Like It* – who sing love songs, are implicitly contrasted with the simple shepherds at Christ's Nativity. Jesus Christ is 'the good shepherd' (John 10:11), echoing 'The Lord is my shepherd' of the Psalms (Psalm 23:1), the original biblical poetry. The poem's title refers to the river crossed by the Israelites in their escape from Egypt into the promised land. It is also where Christ was baptised by John the Baptist. As a **figure** it suggests that the object is to translate (literally carry across) poetry into a new sanctified form which dismisses complication and riddle. It is a poem written in plain vocabulary, its agenda forcefully established by its opening **rhetorical questions**. The poem's **paradox** is, however, that it dismisses its own procedures, for it requires its own riddles to be decoded in order to achieve a reading. The poem, therefore, deletes itself.

7 **arbours** artificial shelters made by training plants over a frame

8 **purling** winding

12 **pull for prime** draw for a winning hand (in the card game of primero)

See also 'Christmas', where the speaker laments his inability to 'sing' God's praises, although his soul is a 'shepherd' (line 17) to the thoughts, words and deeds that serve God and feed on the pasture of his grace.

JORDAN (II)   How to write about God (2)

When I first wrote religious poetry I tried to decorate it as much as possible in order to do justice to its subject. I often made mistakes, but as I worked my own identity became tied up in the labour of writing. Then I heard a voice tell me that all this artificiality was not at all what was required; God's love contains all that needs to be said and needs only to be simply restated.

Like 'Jordan (I)' this is a fundamentally **paradoxical** poem in praise of God, because it rejects poetry as an appropriate vehicle for that praise. The poem is **metatextual** in that its process is its subject. It rejects **metaphor**, yet describes the very compositional process in terms of further metaphors associated with organic growth, 'burnish, sprout, and swell' (line 4), and uses the metaphor of 'Curling' (line 5) to describe the process of metaphor as a **trope**. The first two stanzas not only describe but **parody** how the process of poetic composition becomes obsessed by itself at the expense of its object. The poet too becomes absorbed into the process of composition, and has to retrieve himself and assert that he is distinct from the experience of writing with which he no longer identifies. The Jordan is an **image** of transformation, as it was the river crossed by the Israelites on their flight out of Egypt into the promised land.

The final stanza completes the baptismal process which suggests that poetry should go through a transformation in order to serve God. Like the closing line of John Milton's later **sonnet** 'When I consider how my light is spent', which discusses how he as a blind man can serve God ('They also serve who only stand and wait'), it dismisses as vain and futile any human effort to embellish God's work, and word. The poet becomes copyist, and the reader, distracted by the poem's language, should, it is argued, therefore not read the poem again. The poem expresses a dilemma: the faithful need to articulate praise in order to give expression to their faith, but that process defeats its own object by attracting attention primarily to itself.

3 **quaint** secret, obscure, elaborate
3 **trim** neat, smart
4 **burnish** polish, spread
6 **Decking** decorating
8 **sped** getting on
10 **quick** living, lively
16 *wide* mistaken, wide of the mark

See also 'Aaron', where Herbert expresses the outward duties of the priest in the first stanza, which cover the imperfections of the man described in the second. In 'The Windows' the priest is an imperfect window on God's truth, but his efforts are assisted by the stories fixed in the stained glass windows. The expression of conflict, together with the possibility of a new kind of sanctified expression, is the central **theme** in all Herbert's verse. In 'Denial' the speaker equates alienation from God with discord in his music or poetry, and asks finally that God should help him back, assist him to pray, 'And mend my rhyme' (line 30).

PRAYER (I)   Defining prayer

Prayer can be described only through imperfect comparisons. It defies direct definition, yet is essentially understood.

The poem is a **sonnet** (see Sonnet) constructed entirely from an audacious succession of **metaphors** for prayer, each one replacing the one before, so that the result is a piling up of **connotative** association. There are no verbs, so there is no narrative or argument within the poem, yet it has a process because it works by the accumulation of analogies to arrive at its final half line, which is not a metaphor but an attempt at definition, 'something understood' (line 14).

1 **angels' age** an oxymoron, as angels are eternal

2 **God's breath in man** God breathed life into Adam, the first man

3 **paraphrase** summary of essential elements

4 **plummet** plumb line for measuring straight vertical distances

5 **Engine** artillery

5 **tower** possibly a siege engine for scaling walls, in this case heaven

6 **Christ-side-piercing spear** the blood released when the crucified Christ's side was pierced by the centurion's spear is traditionally the blood of the communion which washes away sin

7 **six-day's world** the earth was created in six days

7 **transposing** changing key (to find new harmony)

10 **manna** the heavenly food with which the children of Israel were fed on their escape from slavery in Egypt, seen by Christians as prefiguring communion bread

11 **ordinary** plain daily normal garb

See also the numerous poems by George Herbert which celebrate and weave metaphors around the individual elements of Christian practice. Notably there are references to the singing of praises in 'Easter' and 'Jordan (I)', to the rituals observed by the priest in 'Aaron', and to elements of the consecrated building in 'The Church-Floor' and 'The Windows'. Many of his poems are prayers in the broadest sense, in that the speaker addresses his communication to God and the reader is cast as an eavesdropper, for example in 'Good Friday', 'The Windows', 'Christmas', 'The Pearl', 'Man', 'Affliction (I)' and 'Denial'.

MAN The world serves humanity enabling humanity to serve God

No one builds a fine house and then does not live in it. Humanity is God's finest creation, containing all that is tree, beast and bird. A human being is a microcosm, as perfectly designed and balanced as the cosmos. Everything in the macrocosm exists to serve us and to be tamed to our use. Having made such a perfect palace as a human being, God should live in it until it lives with him.

By 'Man' we may understand all humankind, although the poet may also be reflecting upon himself as an object of creation. The poem is a straightforward example of the construction of a metaphysical conceit, setting out to prove that the human being as a microcosm contains all the features of the wider universe. That universe conforms to the older earth-centred model, like Donne's in 'The Sun Rising'. The idea that the world was made in the same proportions as the body of a human being, and that the human being is a perfectly balanced state, has sources both in the writings of early Christian Church fathers and in the Roman author Livy, whose vision of the state as an organism was redeployed by Shakespeare in *Coriolanus*. Herbert's human being is also a building, a palace for God, linking the poem to others that use the structure of the church building symbolically, and, unlike classical models of the self-sufficient organism, is vacant until filled by God. References to meat and drink have connotations of the communion during which God's body and blood are eaten and drunk.

17 amity friendship
21 dismount bring down from the heavens (into his eyes)
22 in little in miniature
39 Distinguishèd parted

See also 'The Church-Floor' and 'The Windows', in which the church building as God's house provides metaphors to describe the nature of the relationship between God and humankind. Otherwise the poem, though tonally very different, is reminiscent in its use of metaphysical conceit of John Donne's 'The Flea', in which the marriage of the two lovers is contained within the tiny body of the flea which has sucked both their bloods.

MORTIFICATION
Learn how to die well

Death is the only certainty in life. Infants' swaddling clothes can become their shrouds; young boys asleep in bed speed towards death; young people dance to music reminiscent of the bell that tolls for the funeral; the settled home and family of the middle-aged man encloses him like a grave; the old man moved around in a chair or bed recollects how the coffin will be carried to the grave. Life is spent in anticipation of death: Lord teach us how to die so that all these little dyings will lead us to eternal life.

The poem conforms to an old convention known in Latin as *memento mori*, literally 'remember to die' (see *Carpe Diem* & *Memento Mori*), designed to remind the reader that no one knows when death will come so it is as well to repent now in order to face death in a state of spiritual purity. Here each stanza considers ingeniously how some aspect of each phase of life is suggestive of death. Life is divided into conventional phases, or 'ages': infancy, childhood, youth, middle age and old age. Different traditions see life in anything from three to seven ages. The poem is superficially reminiscent of the speech by Jaques in Shakespeare's *As You Like It* (II.7.166), which suggests that each age of men and women is a part they must play in the drama of life until they end 'Sans teeth, sans eyes, sans taste, sans everything'. Herbert's picture, though grimmer in its reflection that each age carries the prefiguring of death within it, ends on a more optimistic note, suggesting that everything in life is a preparation for death, and that the good death leads to eternal life in heaven. Nor does the division of that life into its phases in the poem make life seem long, but the poem's opening line – 'How soon doth man decay!' – begins the process which collapses each phase into the last, reinforced by the **metaphors** of thawing and melting of the years together in the penultimate stanza. The poem's narrative account of life thus collapses upon itself, ending with the speaker's refusal to assert himself in God's eyes except as a willing candidate for dissolution and death. The poem, therefore, although quieter in **tone**, is comparable in ideological stance to Donne's divine **sonnet** 'Batter my heart, three-personed God', in which he sees

MORTIFICATION continued

dissolution of the self through being ravished by God as the only way to be 'free' (line 13).

2 **sweets** sweet perfumes
5 **clouts** cloths, swaddling clothes
5 **winding sheets** shrouds
17 **knell** the bell rung while someone is dying and after they have died
32 **solemnity** solemn ritual
33 **hearse** framework for supporting a coffin with surrounding candle holders (only latterly a funeral carriage)

See also 'Life', in which the speaker contemplating a fading posy of flowers reflects that if his death comes with such sweetness he will not mind if life is short, and 'Death', in which the hope of the final resurrection of the faithful, body and soul, on Doomsday takes the horror out of bodily decay.

THE PULLEY   The struggle for steadfast faith

When God made man, he endowed him with numerous blessings gathered throughout creation, including strength, beauty, wisdom, honour and pleasure. He stopped short of giving him rest, however, in case he settled back and worshipped himself. He decided to let him keep all the others, but to leave him restless so that if goodness did not turn him to God, weariness might.

The **conceit** (see The Metaphysical Conceit) in this poem involves a complex **paronomasia**, or **pun**, on the word 'rest'. The poem's argument seems to be that when God endowed humanity with blessings, he kept back rest. Consequently we are restless with 'the rest' (in the sense of the remainder). It is this tension between lavish endowment with gifts and lack of contentment that, the poem suggests, pulls humanity back towards God in a state of spiritual exhaustion. So many gifts are likely to make humanity complacent, but sheer weariness, if not innate goodness, will bring the created back to the creator. The process is compared to a pulley, a mechanism for lifting heavy objects using counterweights attached to a rope. The Latin for a pulley is *restis*, hence the pun depends on three meanings for 'rest': 'repose', 'remainder' and 'lifting mechanism'. In addition, the verb 'to tire' has an obsolete meaning, 'to pull', preserved in the modern French *tirer*, so that the poem's title could suggest 'the thing that tires'. The distribution of God's gifts to humanity depends too on the myth of Pandora's box, except that in this instance the gifts do not disperse but, because of a significant omission, prevent humanity's achievement of structured self-sufficiency. The poem is a good example of Herbert's talent for using very plain everyday language with great economy to convey a complex web of ideas.

5 **span** the distance between tip of thumb and tip of little finger across the outstretched palm (approximately twenty centimetres), so a handful, but also possibly suggesting lifespan or humanly limited space and time

8 **made a stay** took a break

14 **Nature** common **personification**, usually as a female, of nature, governing the earthly properties of creation

15 **both** both God and humankind would be diminished if the one was not dependent upon the other

17 **repining** yearning

See also 'The Pearl', where the problems posed in this poem are resolved and in the final stanza the speaker asks God to let down a silk thread to him so that he may climb up to heaven. In 'Life' Herbert uses the stock image of the fading flower to anticipate his own mortality. In 'Affliction (I)' the problem of submission to God's will is turned into a personal narrative. In 'Denial' the speaker, alienated from God, appeals directly to him for an answering voice to 'mend my rhyme' (line 30). Henry Vaughan takes up Herbert's theme of spiritual restlessness in his poem 'Man'.

R‌EDEMPTION   **Christ is crucified daily**

When I had been the tenant of a lord for many years and was not doing well, I decided to go and ask him if I could relinquish the lease and have a new one. I looked for him at his manor, heaven, but was told he had gone to earth to see about some property he had bought there some time ago. I went back and looked for him in all the grandest places but eventually found he had fallen among criminals and been beaten. He granted me my request and died.

The poem is a **sonnet** (see Sonnet) on the subject of the central tenet of Christianity: Christ voluntarily died to redeem the sins of an undeserving humanity. The sonnet takes the form of a **parable** and, like many of the biblical parables, presents God as a feudal overlord and humankind as his tenant. Here the epitome of the whole Christian story, from Adam's loss of the Garden of Eden to Christ's death on the Cross, is rendered **allegorically** in fourteen lines. The speaker represents humanity. His desire for a new cheaper lease represents humanity's situation after the loss of the Garden of Eden, the wish to pay less for Adam's sin and to be accepted into a new and better relationship with God. The second **quatrain** shifts the focus to God, who is absent from heaven, attempting to repossess land on earth which he formerly 'dearly bought' (line 7). The reference is to the Crucifixion by which Christ 'bought' humanity back by paying for Adam's sin with his life, making it possible once more for humanity to go to heaven. The tenant makes the same error as the three wise men at Christ's Nativity, expecting to find him in locations fitting for the rich and famous, but he is instead found under attack and fatally wounded.

The poem is not simply retelling the Christian story, but suggesting that Christ's sacrifice is a repeating event – the land has been 'dearly bought' before. The suggestion is that humanity is perpetually ungrateful for God's overlordship, that consequently Christ is crucified daily, and that his forgiveness is not a single communal historical event but is available in perpetuity to each individual who asks.

3 **make a suit** appeal, put a proposition
10 **resorts** places of social gathering

See also 'Good Friday' for a direct expression of the scale of Christ's sacrifice on the Cross, and 'Easter', which celebrates the Resurrection by calling for music, where the wood of the Cross and the 'stretchèd sinews' (line 11) of Christ provide a model for the poet's lute to accompany a song in praise. In 'The Pearl' Herbert also uses one of Christ's parables, the story in Matthew 13:45–6 of the merchant who sold all he had to buy a pearl of great price. 'Death' describes how physical decay holds no fear for the speaker since humanity's redemption through Christ holds the promise of eternal life. 'Love (III)', more an extended **metaphor** than a parable, develops an imagined dramatic dialogue between the speaker and Love, understood as Christ, where Love offers the speaker hospitality at his table.

THE COLLAR   **Submission to God's will**

I banged on the table and said I'm going out. I'm free. What have I ever got for subjecting myself to God? Nothing but grief. I'll make up for lost time, escape from this cage of my own making, not be scared by thoughts of repercussions any more. But even as I raged, I heard God call me and I replied, 'My Lord.'

Like 'The Pulley', this poem depends upon the **pun** in the title. The collar is part of the harness worn by heavy horses or oxen to pull loads. It is, therefore, emblematic of a loss of freedom, subjugation to a higher power, hard and thankless labour. Spelt differently, 'choler' is a **synonym** for anger. The poem explores the nature of the subjugation of the faithful to God, while simultaneously giving **rhetorical** expression through a succession of questions and exclamations to the feelings of rebellion that God's seeming demand for unquestioning obedience can provoke. The poem's **imagery** draws on the New Testament. The 'thorn / To let me blood' (lines 7–8) may be associated with the crown of thorns placed on Christ's head at the Crucifixion.

1 **board** table
2 **will abroad** want to [go out] into the world
3 **pine** mourn, languish
4 **lines** poetry
5 **store** storehouse, granary
6 **in suit** a supplicant, pleading
8 **let me blood** bleed me (for medicinal purposes)
9 **cordial** soothing medicine
14 **bays** bay leaves (used to crown heroes in the ancient world)
24 **enforce** reinforce, restrain, hold
24 **draw** pull
26 **wink** blink
29 **death's head** skull

GEORGE HERBERT: THE COLLAR continued

See also 'Christmas', where the speaker more submissively from the start offers his 'brutish' soul (line 11) as a refuge for Christ. In 'Affliction (I)' the problem is turned into a personal narrative, telling of how at first faith is a joy, but how it is eroded by sickness and doubt. 'Denial' presents an even more extreme case, and is a direct appeal to God from a speaker alienated from him against his will.

THOMAS CAREW

Most of Carew's surviving poetry concerns the people and occasions with which he was involved as one of Charles I's courtiers. He reworks many conventional themes smoothly and without surprises, but insinuates into his poems new ideas and opinions to suit the taste of the circles in which he moved. His **elegy** (see Lyric) for John Donne shows his work at its best, demonstrating that he could be both intellectually self-aware and a shrewd and direct literary critic.

AN ELEGY UPON THE DEATH OF THE DEAN OF PAUL'S, DR JOHN DONNE

A formal poem of lament on the death of John Donne

Poetry is widowed by the death of Donne. Is anything better than dry prose now possible? Donne's poetry conveyed transcendent emotions to his readers, comparable with the works of great classical poets, because his creativity was fresh and set aside tired conventions. Poetry will now return to verbose reworkings of old tales. The poet asks pardon for breaking with this, his own poor attempt, the silence which, following the death of so great a poet, would be the best **elegy**. Donne the poet provides a **theme** to exhaust all others. On his tomb should be inscribed a reminder that he was the king of all wit, priest both of Apollo, the pagan god of poetry, and of the Christian God.

The poem shows how Carew is aware of his relationship with other writers. He deploys Donne's own favoured fields of **imagery** to characterise the other poet's work. In so doing, although he disparages his own efforts, he shows himself to be an attentive follower and critic. For example, Donne's rejection of the 'soft melting phrases' (line 53) of Elizabethan love poetry is commended through the extended **metaphor** drawn from horticulture, which is, nonetheless, conventional. Donne's characteristic deployment of erotic imagery in religious poetry is captured through the **oxymoron** 'holy rapes' (line 17). The poem also proposes that Donne and poetry are **synonymous**; Donne's wit was more than juggling with words – like the mythological Prometheus it brought fire direct from heaven to burn men's souls. The poem, in foregrounding the process of poetic composition, is full of **irony** and **paradox**. It suggests, in poetry, that after Donne poetry is impossible, and all that is left is the dull prose of funeral orations. It also offers an apology for attempting to follow Donne when silence might be more fitting. Finally, one elegy contains another. The last four lines, written for engraving upon the tomb, move from addressing the dead poet to addressing the passer-by with a reminder of Donne as the universal and quintessential poet.

1 **widowed** suggesting that Donne was married to poetry
4 **dough-baked** stodgy
5 **unscissored** in mourning
13 **frame** give shape to
14 **Grave homilies** sombre moral tales
22 **Delphic** of Apollo, Greek god of music and poetry, whose oracle was situated at Delphi
25 **pedantic** petty, over-correct
25 **weeds** unwanted growth, i.e. bad poetry
27 **servile imitation** slavish adherence to convention
29 **penurious** impoverished
30 **Licentious** audacious
32–3 **Anacreon's ... Pindar's** much imitated early Greek **lyric** poets
40 **Orpheus** the son of Apollo and the muse Calliope, mythical musician
59 **gleanèd** picked up grain after the main harvest is past
70 **apostasy** denial or renunciation of faith
77 **panting numbers** struggling **metre**
87 **engross** gather together
94 **incise** carve

See also Andrew Marvell's 'An Horatian Ode upon Cromwell's Return from Ireland' for a different kind of formal poem celebrating an individual.

Crashaw's work is metaphysical poetry with a difference, being heavily influenced by his Roman Catholicism and his attendant exposure to the aesthetic of the baroque in southern Europe where he lived as a religious exile.

HYMN TO SAINT TERESA

A saint's life

God is Lord of all. To prove that we will tell of his effect on a little girl. Long before she is old enough to understand, she intuitively seeks out death for love of God. It is not to be; Christ saves her for a sweeter martyrdom when he will pierce her heart with flaming darts shot by seraphim, God's soldier angels. When she eventually comes to heaven she will be escorted by the moon to take her place among all shining virginal souls. She will be greeted by angels and she will be crowned with her own good works. Her written works will clothe her in heaven as they continue to inspire us on earth. She will follow in Christ's footsteps in heaven: those who would wish to see her in heaven must live to die as she did.

As the title suggests, the poem is a hymn, offering praise to the saint in direct address. It is also a narrative poem, written in **couplets**, and the events it describes were clearly inspired by the life of St Teresa of Avila (1515–82), founder of the Order of Discalced (barefoot) Carmelites, who was canonised in 1622 by Pope Gregory XV along with the founders of the Jesuit order, Ignatius of Loyola and Francis Xavier. Her autobiography was translated into English and published in 1642 under the title *The Flaming Heart*, for amongst her many reported experiences of spiritual rapture was the 'transverberation' of her heart, the event reported in the poem when her heart is several times shot through with fiery darts from heaven fired by seraphim.

The early sections of the poem demonstrate how she was marked out for a saintly life from early childhood, when she first sought martyrdom by preaching to the Moors. Typically Crashaw depicts a female saint who is feisty in her ardent devotion to Christ. He dismisses male soldierly martyrdom, suggesting that men should learn to copy the fierce love and active submissiveness of this woman. The poem imaginatively constructs the life of St Teresa in heaven, how she was escorted by the 'moon of maiden stars' (line 123). The moon is an **epithet** for the Virgin Mary, often pictured standing on the crescent moon. Here Crashaw develops these conventional comparisons into a shimmering vision of white light, denoting the purity of virgin souls. The language and **imagery** of the poem have a cumulative effect as the narrative progresses, suggestive of the excitement of religious rapture in a manner which is almost sexual.

5 **martyrdom** death for a cause

7 **lusty** vigorous

32 **nonage** minority, being under age

47 **Moors** Muslim inhabitants of North Africa and occupiers of Spain; Catholic Spain's greatest enemy

65 **Spouse** marriage partner; here used of Christ, whose relationship with humanity was conventionally expressed through the **metaphor** of marriage

80 **hallowed** holy, sanctified

94 **seraphims** the highest of the nine orders of angels, military in character, bright red, with six wings apiece

150 **diadems** heavenly crowns

172 **zone** girdle

See also Henry Vaughan's poetry for the use of light imagery to convey the nature of heavenly experience. Crashaw's 'A Hymn of the Nativity, sung as by the Shepherds' makes the conventional singing shepherds of **pastoral** poetry into those who visited Christ at his birth. They too celebrate Christ's birth as the dawning of light into a dark world, and contrast the child's purity with the snow of the first Christmas.

ANDREW MARVELL

Fearsomely scholarly, Andrew Marvell wrote in Latin as well as in English. Some of his poems are inspired by public events of the Civil War period through which he lived, but many are more private. His bookishness is apparent everywhere, but is tempered in his poems of private reflection by a keen and dry wit.

ON A DROP OF DEW

A meditation on the soul, inspired by a dewdrop

Look at how the dew condensing as the sun rises in the east is careless of the rose on which it lands as it is still lamenting and imitating the heavenly sphere from which it came. The sun takes pity on it and breathes it back into the heavens. Such is the human soul, distilled in the body yet remembering where it came from. Thus confined, it moves this way and that, in and out of love, until, like the manna fed to the children of Israel, although it is congealed on earth, it seeks to rise to the sun.

The poem is a meditation on the human soul from the perspective of Neoplatonic philosophy (see Platonic Philosophy). It is characteristically metaphysical in that it begins by comparing a drop of dew on a rose with the spheres of the universe. This dewdrop, poised on a rose – both Christian **symbols** of perfection – is 'Trembling' (line 16) in case it is violated by the world. The human soul, like the dewdrop, is therefore a careless exile on earth. Dewdrops were thought to congeal inside oysters into pearls, and the pearl in the Book of Revelation symbolises the perfect pure soul in heaven. The human being which the soul inhabits is a microcosm, a 'heaven less', standing temporarily in place of the 'greater heaven' (line 26). The two subjects of contemplation, the dewdrop and the human soul, are connected through the **imagery** of condensation and evaporation, drawn from contemporary natural science and biblical **allusion**. The dew is fancifully 'Like its own tear' (line 13), longing to return to the heavens, until the rising sun as part of the normal process of nature reabsorbs it into the atmosphere. The human soul is, by analogy, a restless exile from God, turning this way and that, divided between the darker temptations of the world and the brightness of heaven. It is finally compared to the manna with which God is said in the Old Testament Book of Exodus to have fed the Israelites on their long journey out of slavery in Egypt into the promised land. Manna was dew which congealed as bread, round and white like pearls, then melted when the sun shone on it. The image unites the two subjects of discussion, the dewdrop and the soul, by demonstrating the archetypal Neoplatonic argument that all physical and temporal existence is an exile which contains within it the desire and the possibility of an eventual return to God.

1 **orient** from the east
9 **slight** snub, belittle
23 **swart** black, dark
27 **wound** bound up, enclosed
34 **girt** harnessed, ready

See also 'The Garden', where Marvell uses Neoplatonic philosophy to unite the closely observed world of nature with the immutable and divine. John Donne's 'Twickenham Garden' is a less optimistic meditation upon man's relationship with nature, where unrequited love demands a winter landscape and can 'convert manna to gall' (line 7).

THE NYMPH COMPLAINING FOR THE DEATH OF HER FAWN

The death of a pet: a meditation on the sacrifice of innocence

My fawn is dying because it has been shot by careless soldiers. It was a pointless act, but I would forgive and forget except I fear God will not forget what they have done. The fawn was a pet, a present from my Sylvio, and he has gone too, led by his heart to someone else. After he went the fawn was my only companion and was delightful to me, though, who knows, it might have left me too. But somehow I do not think so, as its love was purer, and I reared it myself. It was prettier and nimbler than any human. It hid in my wilderness garden, where it ate roses and slept among lilies until it took on their properties. Oh help, it is dying quietly and silently weeping. My fawn is dead, but I shall mix its tears with mine and consecrate them to Diana. I shall order it a tomb of white alabaster and die myself.

The poem is a **dramatic monologue** in the voice of the nymph, an **elegy** (see Lyric) to the dying fawn, and also draws heavily on **pastoral tropes,** being set in an idealised wilderness inhabited by the nymph and her faithless shepherd, Sylvio. It imitates a pattern established in both late Latin elegies and earlier English poetry of putting the lament for the death of a pet into the mouth of an innocent girl to affect the reader with a moment of intensely imagined psychological pathos, and then to use it as a springboard into philosophical and religious exploration. This poem depends on an **allusion** to the Latin poet Virgil's *Aeneid*, Book Seven, where Ascanius, son of the warrior prince Aeneas, kills a stag without realising it is the pet of Silvia, the king's gamekeeper's daughter, and thus precipitates war. This is, however, overlaid by imitation of mystical Christian literature in which the soul laments the Crucifixion of Christ as the perfect, virginal, innocent sacrifice.

The poem deploys much religious vocabulary, and the **imagery** of roses and lilies is closely associated with the Virgin Mary, although the poem develops no sequential line of **allegory**. The speaker thus blends the characteristics of a pagan nymph with the suggestion of a female saint, making a reliquary, or sacred vessel, in which to preserve the relics of Christ. Some commentators have suggested that the religious theme is made topical by the reference to 'troopers' (line 1), a reference to 1640 when England was being invaded by the Covenanters, a Scottish Presbyterian army.

 1 **wanton** playful, unruly
 2 **fawn** young deer
 10 **Prevail** influence
 17 **deodands** a personal possession which caused the death of a person and was, consequently, forfeit by law
 24 **offer for their sin** the ignorant troopers have casually killed the one pure thing that might have been sacrificed for their sin
 26 **counterfeit** false, unfaithful
 33 **beguiled** fooled
 34 **waxed** grew
 35 **smart** stinging pain
 69 **hinds** adult deer
 97 **balsam** sap of a tree
 99 **Heliades** in Greek mythology the daughters of Helios, the sun god, who were transformed into trees, and their tears into amber
 104 **Diana's** goddess of hunting and chastity
 107 **Elysium** the Elysian Fields, the classical paradise where souls went after death
 110 **bespeak** place an order to have made

To his coy mistress

On the urgency of desire and the uncertainty of death

If we had all the time and space in the world, your clinging to your virginity would not be a problem. We could pass endless leisure in conversation all over the known world. I could admire each little part of you in turn. But I am always aware that we do not know how much time we have, and when each of us is dead it will be too late for love. So while you are still young and beautiful, let us seize the moment, and if we cannot make time stand still, we'll savour every racing moment of it.

The poem divides clearly into three **verse paragraphs**. In the first the poet **parodies** the **blazon** convention of the love **lyric** (see Love), suggesting that real lovers do not have time to admire each of their lover's constituent parts, but that this is a sort of tortuous foreplay. He uses **hyperbole** to enact the ridiculously unnatural proposition that literary lovers should waste time in conversation and in admiring each other in exotic settings. The deliberate **bathos** of his **juxtaposition** of the Ganges, a very remote site and source of precious stones, with the prosaic Humber – Marvell lived in Yorkshire – serves to illustrate that the voice in the poem is engaged in humorous, if pressing, seduction, and is not to be taken entirely seriously. There are many topical references in this section of the poem: the idea of empire and its extension was a typically European preoccupation in the phase of New World exploration following initial discovery, when the new territories were being consolidated and colonised, while the impossibility of accepting the Jews remained a pressing problem for European Christians until their final readmission to England was accomplished by Oliver Cromwell.

The second paragraph turns from the blazon to deploy another poetic convention: *carpe diem*, Latin for 'seize the day'. This was a common **topos** in religious and moral writing, reminding readers to concentrate on those actions which would benefit their immortal souls, but was less common in love poetry (see *Carpe Diem* & *Memento Mori*). Here Marvell uses a contemplation of the grave which is only semi-serious to remind his lover that if she hesitates further it may be too late for both of them. The mock-lugubrious imagery of the solitude of the grave, with the worms as lovers, draws on well-established, if morbid, moral poems about the horrors of the grave which were designed to frighten the reader into repentance; here, of course, the aim is sexual seduction.

The final paragraph returns to the overriding theme of time, but now refers to the inscrutable movements of the heavens as something that the lovers can influence. Here the poem transcends mechanical poetic convention, as well as the laws of science and nature, by selecting vocabulary which is forthright and sensual, combined with verbs of action, even violence, to promote vigorously the urgency of physical desire.

2 **coyness** physical reticence, bashfulness, reserve

8 **flood** Noah's flood (Genesis 6–9); the very remote past

10 **the conversion of the Jews** some indeterminate future time when Jews might become Christian

22 **Time's winged chariot** the allegorical personification of time sometimes has wings, as in the Latin expression *tempus fugit* ('time flies'), and sometimes, like Helios, or Phoebus, the sun god, rides around the heavens in a chariot

26 **marble vault** underground building for aristocratic family tombs

27 **try** put to the test

29 **quaint** literally proud and old-fashioned, but also possibly a pun on 'queynt', an archaic word for female sexual organs

33 **hue** complexion (some editions have 'glue', in the sense of light moisture)

35 **transpires** breathes through

40 **slow-chapped** slowly devouring

See also 'The Definition of Love', which uses many of the same images of urgency (the verb 'tear') and has much of the energy of 'To his Coy Mistress', but is an altogether more pessimistic poem considering the separation of lovers as the deliberative action of malign fate. 'The Fair Singer' considers the other kind of anguish caused by love, as the speaker is ensnared by a female temptress, based on the sirens from Homer's *Odyssey*, who lured sailors onto the rocks. Thomas Carew's poem 'Persuasions to enjoy' works with the same theme and has a very similar concluding two lines.

THE GARDEN

A country house garden considered as a second Eden

How arrogantly men strive to win wreaths made of the branches of trees, when what plants really do is to encourage retreat from life's efforts. I have found the essence of quiet and innocence in the solitude of the garden, and would rather have a beautiful green plant than a fair woman. In ancient mythology, those pursued frequently turned into plants to escape. The senses are satisfied by an abundance of vegetation, while the mind rises above its common preoccupations and the soul can leave the body behind for a time. It must have been like this in the Garden of Eden for Adam, before the creation of Eve. Even the passage of time seems benign when measured by a sundial designed from flowers and by the industriousness of bees.

The poem invokes the profusion of vegetation to be found in the formal garden of a country house as a remedy for all the stresses of society. The **image** of 'the palm, the oak, or bays' (line 2) – tributes given in the ancient world for military or political achievement – is used **ironically** to demonstrate that the true function of a growing wreath of vegetation is to provide shady repose. Sexual love is also rejected, the conventional red and white of the woman's complexion being dismissed in favour of green. In conventional love poetry, beautiful women's complexions were frequently compared to lilies and roses, their lips to cherries; here the conventional **conceit** is inverted, as vegetation contemplated in solitude itself becomes the lover rather than a storehouse of hackneyed comparisons. The image of lovers carving their names on trees derives from folk custom, but here again there is inversion, as the only wounds inflicted on the trees should be carvings of their own names.

Stanzas four, six, seven and eight muster classical mythology, philosophy and Christian theology to support the argument, while stanza five celebrates the sheer sensuality of a garden in which ripe fruits grow in profusion. Stanza four refers to the Latin poet Ovid's *Metamorphoses*, observing that mythological beings subject to sexual harassment were released by being changed into plants. Stanzas six and seven wittily draw on Neoplatonic philosophy (see Platonic

Philosophy) by proposing that while the body is preoccupied with sensual pleasure the mind can rise up and observe the overarching forms which flow from the deity and dictate the nature of the universe. Thus in the contemplation of these 'other worlds' (line 46) man is united with the mind of God. In this state, the mind releases the soul to commence the Platonic ascent to become one with the deity. The Platonic flight, which is only taken half seriously, then becomes connected to Christian theology in comparing the experience of this garden to the life led by Adam in Eden. In the eighth stanza the speaker reflects that the perfect solitude of Eden, which supplied satisfaction to body, soul and mind, was shattered by the creation of woman long before the Fall. The final stanza returns the reader to earth, but seeks to show how the experience of earthly existence is mediated as something benign by nature, when time is measured by a floral sundial and by the industry of bees.

The poem has no explicit context, but may be connected to the tribute Marvell pays elsewhere to the Parliamentarian general Lord Fairfax's country house at Nun Appleton ('Upon Appleton House'), outside York, where the poet spent time as tutor to Lord Fairfax's daughter immediately after the war.

1 **vainly** futilely

1 **amaze** craze

2 **the palm, the oak, or bays** awards for military, civic and literary achievement in ancient Rome

6 **upbraid** reproach

15 **rude** uncouth

19 **Fond** foolish

25 **run our passion's heat** satisfied our passion

28 **Still** fixed

43 **kind** category in nature

47 **Annihilating** reducing to nothing

51 **vest** garment

54 **whets** preens

60 **meet** equal and fitting

61 **share** deserved lot

66 **dial** sundial

68 **zodiac** the flowers from which the sundial is created form a perfumed
equivalent to the pattern of the heavens

70 **Computes** calculates

See also 'Bermudas', which similarly exults in nature's, and therefore
God's, bounty, but transposes it to the New World. That poem is
framed in a dramatic setting, for it represents a song sung by English
sailors in a small boat and overheard by the narrator. Many sea
shanties wondering at the riches found in the New World as a new
Garden of Eden survive from the period. The 'happy garden-state'
(line 57) is again the theme in 'The Picture of Little T.C. in a
Prospect of Flowers', where inhabiting the garden is equated with
childhood and 'simplicity' (line 1), yet the child, a little girl, endangers
the flowers by plucking the buds, as she will later cause misery and
chaos in love if she survives to adulthood.

HENRY VAUGHAN

Henry Vaughan's poetic output was prolific, but modern commentators
concentrate almost exclusively on the volumes called *Silex Scintillans I* and
II. The poetry in these volumes is heavily influenced ideologically by
Vaughan's devotion to a brand of Anglicanism which sought to return the
Church to a primitive incorrupt condition, and aesthetically to George
Herbert's poetry, which, Vaughan claimed, taught him that the only
function of poetry was to worship God.

REGENERATION

**On the restoration of faith in the individual and purity in
the Church**

I walked out one spring day, but it was winter in my soul because of sin. I
walked on until I reached a summit where there was a set of scales; in one
pan I put my pains, the other my pleasures. I heard someone call to me;
I obeyed the voice and went east into an untrodden field where I found a
grove. Once I was in it everything changed and I found true springtime, but
all was quiet except a fountain playing upon a pool of stones. Then I saw a
bank of flowers, on which were people, some sleeping, some awake. I felt a

wind, but could not see where it came from; it whispered to me so I called out to the Lord asking him to breathe one breath on me so I could die, and regenerate before my life was over. The poem ends on an Old Testament quotation from Song of Solomon 4:16.

The poem describes **allegorically** the process of Vaughan's spiritual rebirth at a moment when he perceives that the world is approaching its end. The wintry **imagery** represents his alienation from God, the discovery of a true spring, hope. He walks east not only because that is where the sun rises and he is anticipating a spiritual dawning, but because it is the traditional location of heaven. The grove he enters is Vaughan's invariable image of the primitive Church in its early days during Christ's own lifetime with his apostles, the woodland setting of pagan worship converted to Christianity free of the buildings and ceremony of the developed Church. But this Church is already full of sluggish people, which is how the poet's politics characterised the revolutionary Church of his own time. It is not, therefore, a return to Christ's lifetime, but an anticipation of the Second Coming of Christ which will herald the end of the world, the apocalypse. The fountain, drawn from John 4:14, is a traditional mystic symbol for the grace of God made available to humanity through Christ's sacrifice on the Cross, but commentators are unable to agree about the meaning of the stones. The poet characterises himself as willing to be chosen by God, the 'rushing wind' referring to Acts 2:2.

'Regeneration' comes at the beginning of the first volume of *Silex Scintillans*, Vaughan's collection of religious **lyric** verse. The whole work represents a conversion experience, but it remains a matter for debate whether Vaughan was regenerated by religious conversion, or whether the process is principally a literary experience. This poem shows considerable consciousness of poetic technique; the crafting of the stanza form and the packing of each line with **connotative** vocabulary, despite its apparent narrative shape, all suggest a poet anxious to cast off 'bonds' (line 1), to experiment with new ways of writing. The subject is spiritual, and there are many biblical echoes, but the final quotation is from the Bible's own great poem, the Song of Solomon, itself read as an allegorical love song of Christ for the Church.

1 **ward** in the care of a guardian; or, in an older sense, a prisoner

1 **bonds** fetters

2 **stole abroad** escaped secretly into the world

9 **Stormed** battered by storms

9 **straight** immediately

10 **stage** false, artificial

24 **heavier grains** former self-indulgence weighs heavier than the pains of his purgatorial journey

28 **Jacob's bed** Genesis 28:10–22, the location of his dream of a ladder going to heaven

33 **reposed** rested

34 **descried** perceived

41 **unthrift** extravagant

54 **cistern** collecting pool below a fountain

80 ***Where I please*** wherever I want to

See also 'The Morning-watch', which also equates the early morning with spiritual and poetic rebirth. 'The Dawning' looks forward more explicitly to the Second Coming of Christ, meditating on what time of day is most appropriate for Christ to return to earth. 'Cock-crowing', from the second volume of *Silex Scintillans*, draws on Herbert's 'Love (I)' and 'Love (II)', as well as Thomas Vaughan's theological works, to fashion another poem of apocalyptic meditation. *Silex Scintillans* as a collection is arranged around the passage of the day, echoing the cycle of prayers in the monastic hours which begins with matins and ends with compline, the service of the night.

THE WORLD   **Humanity needs to leave worldly occupation and look upwards**

I had a vision of the universe as a huge glowing ring, spinning and controlling the earth at the centre, and on the earth a sad lover contemplating a single flower. The statesman too moved sluggishly amongst a discontented people, like a mole hunting underground, his corruption fed by established institutions. Greed caused many to focus on material things and earthly comfort. Some did attempt to worship God, but were benighted. There is a way to the heavens, but the universe's shining ring is available only to the true bride of the bridegroom.

THE WORLD continued

This visionary poem has a famous opening line, arrestingly **juxtaposing** eternity with a single casual moment: 'the other night'. The poem's **imagery** depends on the old model of the universe as a series of concentric spheres containing heavenly bodies, whirling around the earth at their centre. The conjunctions of the planets in their spheres – the zodiac – govern linear time and decay, to which only the earth is subject. The perception of the world as an imperfect mutable reflection of the heavens draws on Neoplatonic philosophy (see Platonic Philosophy). Here the whirling bright universe is explicitly the way to heaven, a '*ring*' which the bridegroom, Christ, reserves for his '*bride*' (lines 59–60), the true Church, according to mystic imagery which draws on the Song of Solomon in the Old Testament and the **apocalyptic** vision at the end of the New Testament, Revelation, where those saved in heaven for ever are described as the brides of the Lamb, Christ.

The middle of the poem is taken up with describing those who never look up to heaven but are preoccupied by earthly things, perhaps echoing the conventional 'ages of man': youth, preoccupied with earthly love, middle age with earthly power and old age with worldly goods. The contemporary Church is bound up with those who do not reach for heaven. It is an instrument of the statesman – a reference to what Vaughan sees as the inappropriate political role of the Church in the Civil Wars – from which some have found a way to heavenly comfort, but in which many remain earthbound. The end of the poem seems to retreat from expanding the imaginary vision and its potentially **satirical** attack on the world, however, as if the poet remembers that such an assertion of superiority is vanity and that the eternal destiny of all, including himself, is God's alone to judge and dispose.

7 **train** followers
8 **quaintest strain** most obscure or ingenious song
21 **without** outside
23 **lest** in case
37 **pelf** treasure
38 **epicure** follower of Epicurus's philosophy of self-indulgence and sensuality
51 **grots** grottoes, rough stone shelters

See also 'The Night' for imagery which suggests that the heavens can be seen only imperfectly from earth. The suggestion that experiencing life on earth leads to an alienation from God and a spiritually unhealthy attachment to transient material things is the theme also of 'The Retreat', where early childhood is presented, using the same **metaphor**, as a journey away from God, heaven and pure light. 'The Waterfall' uses a whole poem to demonstrate how heaven may be glimpsed through the contemplation of its reflection in a single aspect of the created world.

MAN   **In all creation, only human beings struggle with God**

Humble things on earth, the bees, birds and flowers, go about their lives according to natural rhythms, apparently unconscious of their relationship with the eternal. They lack man's sophistication but are sustained in their untroubled existence by God. Human beings by contrast are restless, forever chasing after worldly things. Consciousness rewards humanity with the knowledge of heaven, but not of how best to get there. Human beings, therefore, behave like the shuttle in a loom, moving as God ordains and unable to rest.

The poem uses the idea of the chain of being, a hierarchical structure in which humanity is above stones, plants and animals but below the angels, to demonstrate how the lower orders of creation lead a life in closer harmony with God than can human beings. The pattern of the day from dawn to dusk is marked out by appropriate behaviour from creatures not capable of exercising independent will and reason. They are rewarded by being splendidly provided for by God, and here the poem refers to Matthew 6:28–9, where it is said that Solomon, the greatest king of Israel, was not decorated by God as beautifully as the lilies which do nothing in return. Yet, the speaker observes, humanity is apparently condemned to constant striving. The **imagery** of incessant motion is used to demonstrate humanity's lack of a sense of God, and heaven as the true destination, 'home' (line 19). It is further suggested that stones, simply by lying on the ground, point to heaven, demonstrating that they understand where their home is.

The poem closes with an extended **conceit** (see The Metaphysical Conceit) which compares humanity to the shuttle in a loom, the moving part whose function is to rush to and fro in the cloth of creation, prevented from rest because of how God made us. The use of the chosen stanza form serves the poem's **epigrammatic** climax well. In each stanza the final three lines give an example or reinforcing statement which bears out the assertion of the first four; in the final stanza the break before the conceit is more emphatic as the fifth line has an irregular **metre**, beginning with a stressed instead of an unstressed syllable, emphasising 'Man' (line 26) in opposition to the 'God' which opens the final line.

2 **mean** humble

4 **intercourse** exchange, conversation

7 **bowers** arches of vegetation

10 **cleave** cling on

15 **toys** diversions

15 **care** anxieties, responsibilities

26 **shuttle** the device used in weaving to carrying the weft or woof threads through the fixed warp as cloth is woven on a loom

27 **looms** the fixed frame in which cloth is woven

See also Andrew Marvell's poem 'The Garden' and John Donne's 'A Nocturnal upon St Lucy's Day, being the shortest day' for very different poems which use the **paradox** that created things lower down the chain of being than humanity can still be in greater harmony with God. George Herbert in 'Jordan (II)' demonstrates that God does not need his own gifts back in the form of human endeavour. However, the greatest influence on this poem is Herbert's 'The Pulley', which expresses through a single conceit the suggestion that to live on earth in conscious knowledge of the existence of God is to live in a constant state of spiritual restlessness and conflict.

PART THREE

CRITICAL APPROACHES

THE METAPHYSICAL CONCEIT

Samuel Johnson gave a useful definition of the metaphysical **conceit** as *discordia concors*, that is the assertion that things apparently quite dissimilar are alike. It was the so-called New Criticism of the mid twentieth century, privileging the study of texts as something essential and transcending the culture in which they were generated, which used the occurrence of this type of comparative device to develop the category 'metaphysical poetry'. The critic K.K. Ruthven (Ruthven, 1969) uses John Milton's definition of the conceit to suggest that it is 'a disjunct similitude with its emphasis on proportion and reciprocity of parts'. The ancient Greek philosopher Aristotle in his *Poetics* set up the idea that there might be a scale of far-fetchedness in the construction of **metaphors**, and it is clear that what the metaphysical conceit does is to exploit the extreme end of that scale for dramatic effect. It is this extremity which leads to the conceit being associated with 'wit', in its original sense of 'quick-wittedness' rather than necessarily humorous.

There is something distinctive in the way a conceit is used too. Metaphor and **simile** in poetry imply comparison, but the reader is left alone to accept or reject the comparison. The author of a metaphysical conceit, however, sets out to prove the justness of an improbable comparison. John Donne's famous comparisons of himself and his mistress first with gold leaf and then with a pair of compasses in 'A Valediction: forbidding Mourning' are extended similes. But it is the far-fetchedness of the objects chosen for comparison, together with the **rhetorical** structure of this section of the poem as persuasive argument, which makes the conceits. Similarly, Donne's 'Good Friday, 1613. Riding Westward' opens with the declaration: 'Let man's soul be a sphere', drawing on the manner in which a mathematical proof is constructed using algebra, where the reader is required to allow that certain ciphers stand for physical quantities.

The association of the metaphysical with the conceit arose in the period when these poets were writing. The Scots writer William Drummond of Hawthornden commented on poets making use of

'Metaphysical Ideas' (see Gardner, 1957). Later Samuel Johnson again objected to the inclusion of philosophical ideas in love poetry rather than affecting images drawn from nature. It is not simply the far-fetchedness of the comparisons that makes for metaphysical conceit, but the areas of human thought and experience which are drawn on to supply the comparisons. Metaphysical conceits take those attributes which are classically associated with the heart – love and devotion – and unite them with the intellectual topics which excited seventeenth-century thinkers, such as science, geography, cosmography and mathematics.

FORM

LYRIC

Many of the well-known poems in anthologies of metaphysical poetry may be categorised as songs and sonnets, the title given to John Donne's collected love poems by an early editor. Song, or more commonly lyric in literary terminology, is a slippery term, often used to mean little more than a shortish poem, usually about love, and possibly, but not always, written for setting to music. The tradition of English lyric verse dates back to the Middle Ages. It is generally written in syllabic metre and rhymed, sometimes in complex shapes. Sometimes it is written as if in the personal voice of the poet, but it may adopt a dramatic voice or voices. It employs a number of literary devices to impart emotion. Lyric verse is often occasional – written for a specific historical moment, event or person – and survives in a number of contexts including manuscripts for private circulation.

Elegy describes any poem lamenting loss, usually the death of a single identifiable person. Carew's 'An Elegy upon the Death of the Dean of Paul's, Dr John Donne' is the most formal and sustained example of elegy studied here, written in rhymed couplets of iambic pentameters. Most of the elegies studied in this Note, however, are formally indistinguishable from lyrics. They are short verses conforming to a variety of verse forms, elegies only in so far as their subject matter deals with loss. The pattern poem is another specialised subset of the lyric. Writing poems whose external shape on the page presents a visual image relating to the subject of the verse, like George Herbert's 'Easter wings' (see Extended

Commentaries), was adopted from the ancient Greeks and was very popular in the Early Modern period. George Puttenham, who wrote *The Arte of English Poesie* in 1589, saw physical arrangement on the page as a legitimate element in poetic composition. In metaphysical poetry the pattern can be treated as a visual **conceit**, in that it expresses succinctly and by imitation some emblematic dimension of the poem's meaning.

Sonnet

The **sonnet** is a specialised subset of the **lyric**, a specific and exacting form which was introduced into English from Italian in the early 1500s and has never lost popularity. The first English sonneteers were aristocrat poets Sir Thomas Wyatt and Henry Howard, Earl of Surrey, who wrote in the reign of Henry VIII. They both translated some of the love sonnets of the Italian poet Francis Petrarch, as well as naturalising the form into English. Shakespeare wrote numerous sonnets, and by the time John Donne was writing the form was thoroughly anglicised.

All sonnets have fourteen lines, generally **iambic pentameters**. The classic Italian or Petrarchan sonnet divides into an **octave**, the first eight lines, then a **sestet**, the final six. The octave rhymes abba abba; the sestet has c, d and e rhymes in one of a number of combinations. The Shakespearean sonnet, on the other hand, divides into three **quatrains** (four lines) and a **couplet** (two lines) and rhymes abab, cdcd, efef, gg. There are, of course, many variations on these two basic shapes, as the form developed through numerous experiments. The divisions are not mechanical, and the best sonneteers exploit the extreme rigour of the form. The Petrarchan sonnet allows for a dramatic reversal or revision of argument after the eighth line, whereas the Shakespearean sonnet develops its argument at a more leisurely pace over the three quatrains only to turn it on its head in the **epigrammatic** final two lines. John Donne uses the Petrarchan form in his *Holy Sonnets*, but also always concludes each one with a rhyming couplet. Understanding how the sonnet form works helps the reader to divide apparently difficult poems, like George Herbert's 'Redemption', into constituent parts, and can be a great help in structuring close textual analysis.

LOVE

It rather states the obvious to point out that love is a major **theme** in metaphysical poetry. It is important nonetheless to look closely at how these poems express sentiment and how they situate the lover and the object of affection. Short love poems in English from the time of Chaucer onwards are associated with the leisured classes, often the immediate court circle, and belong to a category of poetry called *vers de société* – the 'verse of (high) society'. Whether they were written by professional court poets and minstrels or by literary young men about town, it is dangerous to assume that seemingly personal expressions of emotion are addressed to real lovers; they can be compliments to influential people or simply exercises in a particularly refined type of expression.

The speaker is almost always male, addressing or talking about his lover in a particular way. One of the conventional ways of setting about writing a **Renaissance** love poem is called the **blazon**, after the technique in heraldry of listing significant parts of a coat of arms. In blazon verse the lover anatomises his love, listing off the parts of her body and comparing each with either beautiful things in nature or precious stones. Thomas Carew's 'A Song', which begins: 'Ask me no more where Jove bestows, / When June is past, the fading rose', is a classic example of the exercise of blazon poetry. Its persistence and formulaic nature also lead to **parody**. Shakespeare famously begins Sonnet 130: 'My mistress' eyes are nothing like the sun; / Coral is far more red than her lips' red' and ends by declaring that she is far more lovely than any of the precious objects with which he might quite inaccurately compare her. Andrew Marvell does not question the accuracy of conventional comparison in 'To his Coy Mistress', but there he too overturns the convention by suggesting that it is a waste of valuable loving time to describe the lover's constituent parts in detail. In another poem, 'The Garden', in which he celebrates the value of solitude, he is able to refer very economically to his preference for nature over woman by extolling the virtues of green over red and white. John Donne in 'Elegy: To his Mistress Going to Bed' celebrates not her body parts but each item of clothing, provided she removes it.

The popularity of John Donne's love poetry rests chiefly on its erotic **imagery**, which gives it an immediacy accessible to modern readers. He is not the first English poet to write erotic love poetry, however; many of Shakespeare's **sonnets** celebrate physical love, and Sir Thomas Wyatt in a poem beginning 'They flee from me' recollects not the formal beauty of his lost lover but her bare arms and shoulders on one particular moment when she came to him in his chamber at night. Many Renaissance love poems never arrive at the moment of consummation, however, but are expressions of the pain of lost or unrequited love. There are also conventional forms of expression in these poems, as the lover experiences symptoms of physical illness, often compared to extremes in the weather, as a result of insupportable separation from his lady. Thomas Carew in 'Mediocrity in Love Rejected' wallows in the pain of rejection, delighting in 'The torrid, or the frozen zone' (line 2). John Donne's 'Twickenham Garden' eloquently expresses how everything is blighted by disappointment in love. In that poem the landscape he describes is not in tune with his feelings (**pathetic fallacy**), although he strongly feels it ought to be. Donne's poetry of separation in love generally strikes a different note, however, as it is about the forced separation of two lovers by travel or by death. In poems such as 'A Valediction: forbidding Mourning' and 'The Relic' he uses both Platonic and Christian philosophy, as well as ingenious **conceits**, to find consolation in the view that physical separation is irrelevant when two lovers' souls are fused.

Where is the woman in all this poetry about men in love? Although she is not always and only a list of body parts, she is identified generally as the other, the person subject to the love of the speaker. The choice of those images of comparison and contrast which make these poems so vivid cannot and does not reflect modern gender consciousness, any more than the poets' enthusiastic admiration of foreign conquest and colonisation accords with later attitudes to empire building. Consequently Donne's portrayal of himself as conqueror and his mistress as territory in 'The Sun Rising' and again in 'Elegy: To his Mistress Going to Bed', or of his mistress as fixed while he roves in 'A Valediction: forbidding Mourning', accords with the values of the culture of his time.

We do well to remember that not all English Renaissance love poetry was written by men and for women. A number of Shakespeare's love sonnets were written to a young male friend, and Katherine Philips wrote to a close female friend, lamenting their forced separation as their marriages removed them to different parts of the country (see Extended Commentaries). Although Philips is often unoriginal, and admires and copies Donne's images, in her poems we witness an equality and mutuality in love. She also wrote a poem for her son Hector who died in infancy, which is a different kind of **elegiac** poem of separation in love. Indeed the imagery associated with love is not confined to sexual or even human love, but is transposed to great effect into some of the religious verse of the period. John Donne famously asks God to 'Batter my heart', and the devotional poems of George Herbert and Henry Vaughan are intensely personal explorations of the love relationship between the individual and his God.

RELIGION & THE CHURCH

Conflicting religious beliefs and ecclesiastical organisations were fundamental features of early seventeenth-century English culture, so inevitably they supplied a major **thematic** area in the imaginative writing of the period. Modern readers of this poetry, without necessarily becoming expert theologians, need to be aware that it is probably inadequate to describe the poems in the collection which deal with eternal themes as simply 'devotional' without having some awareness that every expression of religious sentiment in this period was carefully and politically modulated (see Religion and Politics).

Ever since the anonymous medieval **lyricist** wrote: 'I sing of a maiden / That is makeless' (a **pun** suggesting, all at once, without a mate, a spot, or an equal), addressing his love song to the Virgin Mary, the **imagery** of love poetry and that of religious verse have interpenetrated each other. John Donne teeters on the edge of blasphemy in 'The Canonization', where he equates the exalted nature of pure sexual love with the spiritual attainments of the saints, and equally when he finishes a **sonnet** addressed to God ('Batter my heart, three-personed God') asserting, 'Except you'enthral me, never shall be free, / Nor ever chaste, except you ravish me'. The critic who believes that poetry communicates the essential individual personality of the poet doubtless would go no further than to see both these examples as the products of a particularly intense temperament. Trends in current criticism would, however, explain the apparently personal nature of seventeenth-century religious verse from a different starting point.

Lutheran Protestantism (see Religion) provides us with the first fundamental explanation for the apparently personal nature of Early Modern devotional poetry. Luther asserted that humanity attained salvation not primarily through the intervention of the Church or the saints, but was justified by faith alone. In other words, the individual Christian was released from the requirement to use the priesthood as an intermediary to form a direct relationship with God. The other major figure of the northern European Reformation was John Calvin, whose most influential doctrine was predestination. According to Calvin, everyone was predestined to go to either heaven or hell, and a person's behaviour in this life was not so much about earning a place in the hereafter as demonstrating symptoms of predetermined election or damnation. John Donne in his *Holy Sonnets* demonstrates a pervasive, almost neurotic, concern with whether he may already be damned (see for example 'At the round earth's imagined corners').

John Donne is also scrupulous in his poetry to reject the trappings of the discredited Roman Catholic faith, referring openly to the 'mis-devotion' (line 13) of worshipping the relics of saints in 'The Relic'. He may evoke the standard pictorial image of Christ's Passion, familiar in Roman Catholic art, in 'Good Friday, 1613. Riding Westward', but it is an image in his mind's eye only. A marked contrast is Roman Catholic convert Richard Crashaw's 'Hymn to Saint Teresa'. This poem, which he wrote in exile in Italy, is a rapturous example of the narration of the life of a recently canonised saint (hagiography), and as such would have been unthinkable in the English context of his day.

George Herbert and his disciple in religious writing, Henry Vaughan, are the most difficult to characterise in terms of devotional ideology. Both essentially Anglicans, they were moderates in the volatile ecclesiastical world of their time. Vaughan subscribed to a particularly obscure subset of Anglican beliefs, however, seeking a return of the national Church to an incorrupt primitive condition which he believed to have existed in the early Celtic Church. Vaughan expresses this view most clearly, along with a rejection of the ecclesiastical radicals of his day who lie in a torpor, alienated from God, in 'Regeneration'.

It is Herbert, ostensibly the most straightforward, who has caused the greatest critical controversy, however. Clearly Protestant, he steadfastly addresses his personal relationship with God in his poems. It has become almost a cliché to talk of his 'plainness'. In 'Jordan (I)' and 'Jordan (II)' he promotes biblical text as the primary, possibly the only, acceptable **discourse** of the faith. Yet other poems in *The Temple* speak from the point of view of the Anglican middle way, where decoration of the church is a fitting element in preaching, teaching and showing respect for God, provided it keeps on the right side of idolatry. This is evident in 'The Windows', which eloquently justifies the use of stained glass. Important critical analyses have demonstrated evidence in Herbert's poetry for a consideration of Calvinist beliefs (see Lewalski, 1979), and many poems, for example 'The Collar' and 'The Pulley', can be read as expressions not only of the difficulty of submitting to divine will, but also of an underlying anxiety that spiritual rebelliousness might be symptomatic of a predestined damnation.

*C*ARPE DIEM & MEMENTO MORI

Less a **theme** than a **topos**, the Latin expression *carpe diem* – literally 'seize the day' – is used to describe the conventional preoccupations many Early Modern poems demonstrate with the passage of time and the unpredictability of death. The common location for such sentiments is in the dreary little poems sometimes found on tombstones reminding passers-by that they too will die, possibly sooner than they imagine. *Carpe diem* is a convenient call to repentance for the preacher too. The sentiment survives more positively in popular **aphorisms** such as 'Eat, drink and be merry, for tomorrow we may die' and 'Make hay while the sun shines'. It is this call to opportunism that Thomas Carew employs in the first stanza of 'Persuasions to enjoy', in which 'Celia' is reminded that her attractiveness, and therefore the prerogative to choose whom and when she loves, will not last for ever. In this poem the second stanza changes tack and suggests that far from being mortal and limited, her charms are eternal and limitless, so she need have no fear that using them will use them up. Andrew Marvell in 'To his Coy Mistress' goes further, suggesting that if the lady hesitates to lose her virginity, she may end up with worms as her only bedfellows.

The other side to *carpe diem* is *memento mori*, or 'remember you must die'. Poetry uses this topos not as encouragement to lead this life to the full, but rather to move readers to repent their sins in anticipation of experiencing the joys of eternal life in heaven. George Herbert's 'Life' sees in a fading posy of flowers 'Time's gentle admonition' (line 9), and confirms that he will 'follow straight without complaints or grief' (line 16), because if he is sweet to God he has no need to care if his life is short. In 'Mortification' he, apparently morbidly, connects some dimension of each phase in a person's life to the experience of death, only to finish by reflecting that whenever death comes, if we die well, there is the promise of eternal life. That promise, for the Christian, derives from Christ's sacrifice on the Cross, which, according to Herbert's 'Death', put the blood back in death's face with the promise of bodily resurrection for all on Doomsday. John Donne too, in the sonnet 'Death be not proud', argues that death is impotent for the Christian because of the promise of the final resurrection of the dead on Doomsday.

PLATONIC PHILOSOPHY

The Early Modern period rediscovered Plato in the original Greek, so Platonic ideologies gained a new fashionability. According to Platonic philosophy, the observable world is subject to change and decay, and where people and things represent qualities, such as beauty, they do so imperfectly. The essence of these qualities, or 'forms' as Platonic philosophy calls them, lies not in the observable world but in the permanent and unchanging world of the deity. Although Plato himself pre-dated Christianity by a number of centuries, the convergent nature of his philosophical universe with a single godhead embodying perfection fitted well with Christian thought. The combination of Platonism with oriental mysticism, originating at Alexandria in the third century after Christ's birth, is known as Neoplatonism ('neo' meaning 'new'). Neoplatonism suggests that the human soul falls away from its true centre in the Godhead to the imperfect world of matter. This both draws on Plato's original theory of forms and accords with New Testament teaching on the relation between God and the human world.

For John Donne, Neoplatonic philosophy provides the consolation that, although lovers are separated either by distance ('A Valediction: forbidding Mourning') or death ('Since she whom I loved hath paid her last debt'), it is only in this 'Dull sublunary' world that physical separation has meaning ('A Valediction: forbidding Mourning', line 13). In 'The Garden'

Marvell, on the other hand, suggests that the setting and his own solitude
allow the speaker's soul to escape the body for a time and soar upwards
towards God. For George Herbert the struggle between striving against
and accepting God's will, between doubt and faith, is presented through
metaphors of being pulled up and down ('The Pulley') or of flight ('Easter
wings'). Henry Vaughan's 'The World' presents the world as an imperfect
mutable reflection of the heavens; the whirling bright universe around and
above it is the way to heaven. In 'Man' he discusses how humans are higher
up the chain of being, a Neoplatonic description of the hierarchy of created
things, yet because we are endowed with reason we cannot unquestioningly
and steadfastly worship God as the stones and beasts do. The **imagery**
of these and many other poems of the period, both devotional and secular,
demonstrates the influence of Neoplatonism on seventeenth-century
thought and on the shaping of poetic **discourse**

LANGUAGE & STYLE

JOHN DONNE

Paradox is at the centre of Donne's repertoire of figures of thought and
speech. He is consistently self-contradictory: 'Those are my best days, when
I shake with fear' ('Oh, to vex me', line 14). Just as we now know that he
composed erotic poetry and devotional poetry at every period in his creative
life, we have to recognise the recurrence of **images** based upon the
irresolvable tension between the sexual and the spiritual, the desire to
move east while 'carried towards the west' ('Good Friday, 1613. Riding
Westward', line 9). The temptation to read this struggle, actually
articulated in carefully crafted formal structures of comparison and
contrast like the **metaphor** and the **simile**, as the outburst of an impulsive
personality arises from other features of Donne's characteristic style. He is
assertive, even with God: 'Batter my heart, three-personed God'; he can be
colloquial: 'Busy old fool, unruly sun' ('The Sun Rising', line 1); 'For God's
sake hold your tongue, and let me love' ('The Canonization', line 1). He
protests against injustice with **rhetorical questions** which brook no
contradiction: 'What merchant's ships have my sighs drowned?' ('The
Canonization', line 11) or pleads for attention: 'Let me pour forth / My

tears before thy face, whilst I stay here' ('A Valediction: of Weeping',
lines 1–2). He can be devastated by grief:

> Study me then, you who shall lovers be
> At the next world, that is, at the next spring:
>> For I am every dead thing,
>>>> ('A Nocturnal upon St Lucy's Day, being the shortest day', lines 10–12)

and is, above all, emotional: 'Blasted with sighs, and surrounded with tears,
/ Hither I come to seek the spring' ('Twickenham Garden', lines 1–2).

We should beware of reading these poems with 'attitude' as clues to
the impetuous personality of John Donne; rather we should look at how
John Donne the poet uses, for example, the **imperative mood** of the verb
in particular to create the illusion of an individuated dramatic voice, seeking
the reader's, or the lover's – or God's – attention. In this way he creates a
sense of urgency in what he has to say.

The illusion is that the speaker is often verging on loss of emotional
control, yet this belies the fact that Donne's writing is very controlled. This
can be observed particularly in his ability to render preposterous arguments
plausible:

> since thy duties be
> To warm the world, that's done in warming us.
> Shine here to us, and thou art everywhere;
> This bed thy centre is, these walls, thy sphere. ('The Sun Rising', lines 27–30)

After the bluster of imperatives and protests, the simple **declarative
sentences** give the illusion of a gained insight, of calm, logical progression,
capable of making the most improbable assertions acceptable for the
duration of the poem.

The alternation of sentence structures, using different moods of the
verb and alternating between simple and complex **syntax**, is one feature of
Donne's style. Another is his choice of vocabulary which observes no rules
of **register** but rather yokes together for effect the sublime with the obscure,
the technical and the colloquial. All these effects draw on the ancient art of
rhetoric, devised as a system of rules governing public speech and writing
in the ancient world, but equally applicable to all utterances in which form
is an important element in the construction of meaning. The classical art of
rhetoric promoted the art of persuasive language; Donne uses many of

those tricks of persuasion while observing rhetoric's first rule, which is to *appear* completely spontaneous.

GEORGE HERBERT

George Herbert's titles repay attention. Frequently they are like crossword clues, and establish with the economy of that most English of **tropes**, the **pun**, networks of comparison which are teased out in the poems. The vocabulary of the poems themselves is simple to the point of austerity, and needs little glossing for the modern reader. It owes much to the seventeenth-century translation of the Bible into English, the so-called Authorised Version, which, although it is celebrated as 'poetic' by modern readers, strove to achieve a plain and unassuming style at the time. Just as the English version of the Lord's Prayer contains only two non-Anglo-Saxon words, 'temptation' and 'trespasses', so too Herbert uses neutral everyday words, sparingly supplemented with English derived from Church Latin.

Similarly, the **connotative** properties of Herbert's **imagery** depend on biblical reference, as in 'Redemption' or 'The Pearl', or on the objects and furnishings which are the physical trappings of churches and worship, such as are found in 'The Church-Floor' and 'The Windows'. Otherwise he draws upon areas of common experience which any country parson might find around him and build into sermons accessible to the simplest parishioner: flowers, trees, herbs, stars and music.

Apparently neutral vocabulary and a certain quietness of tone belie the difficulty and the intensity of Herbert's verse, much of which deals as urgently with inner conflict as John Donne's, though in a style as introverted as Donne's is flamboyant. Herbert's verse is economical to a fault, so that spiritual conflict and rebellion may be expressed simply by an alternation of long and short lines. This minimalist, 'designer' quality in his poems is best illustrated by 'Easter wings', where meaning is ultimately expressed by the shape the words form upon the page, but is mirrored by the unavoidable swell and fall of the voice when the poem is read aloud. Herbert's verse is no less dramatic than Donne's, even though the style is even and austere. The poems present a voice in conflict, sometimes with God, sometimes with itself, so that we are asked to accept a dramatic volte-face at the end of 'The Collar', as protest is quelled, or to feel the constant

competing tugs of heaven and earth in 'The Pulley'. It is in keeping with
the unease of this pent-up poetic voice that it should slide into **irony**,
another very English trope, to create unease in the reader as well as to
expose the speaker's inadequacies. Hence in 'Easter' the joyful hymn-like
opening, welcoming the risen Lord, is thoroughly undermined by the
recognition that Christ 'wast up by break of day, / And broughtst thy sweets
along with thee' (lines 21–2). Indeed irony is a powerful tool used to root
out any attention-seeking inclinations in the overeager worshipper, when,
as we find in God's voice in 'Jordan (II)':

> *There is in love a sweetness ready penned:*
> *Copy out only that, and save expense.* (lines 17–18)

God, who is self-evidently self-sufficient, does not need his gifts
represented to him, and that includes the gift of poetry.

Henry Vaughan

In many respects Henry Vaughan is Herbert's imitator, and a number
of his poems show the clear influence of Herbert, but stylistically
the difference is unmistakable. Both repudiated what they saw as the
extravagances of secular love poetry. In Herbert this generated an
economical, pent-up style, crafted from the play on meaning available from
stark common vocabulary. Vaughan, who unlike Herbert experienced the
social upheaval of the Civil Wars, rather sought a new primitivity to give
poetry an authority to match the times in which the old courtly values had
been swept aside. In his poetry the self is in retreat, a retreat from
engagement with society, but not a retreat from the sensory experience of
the observable world. Vaughan's return to the primitive amounts to a
renegotiation of the relationship of the self with God and with the
phenomena of the created universe. This is expressed as the experience of
discoveries to be exclaimed at, and through a vocabulary of intense
extremes. Personal spiritual experience fluctuates between the fulfilment
available through God's love and the total annihilation of alienation from
God, so that in 'Cock-crowing' sleep without God becomes a death, not
just of body but of spirit:

> To sleep without thee, is to die;
> Yea, 'tis a death partakes of hell:

> For where thou dost not close the eye
> It never opens, I can tell.
>   In such a dark, Egyptian border,
>   The shades of death dwell and disorder. (lines 25–30)

When he is describing phenomena in the world, they take on a transcendent specialness which has led to Vaughan being compared with the early nineteenth-century Romantic poets. The whole first stanza of 'The Waterfall' not only conveys the liquidity of the waterfall itself through the m and l and s sounds, but also animates that liquidity with its 'murmurs' and by having it 'chide' and 'call' (lines 1 and 4). Where Herbert is terse in his desire not to be showy, Vaughan will use multiple adjectives and verbs to accumulate the precise sensory or mystical experience in the texture of his text. Units of **syntax** – phrases, clauses and sentences – are longer than in Herbert's verse and the structure is looser, but there is no sacrifice of control, rather an accumulated verbal energy, a sense of flight. Vaughan constantly returns to the **imagery** of light, and all the properties of bright light, reflected light, obscured light, shadow, flame and pitch darkness recur in his poems to communicate the experience of alienation from and fusion with God, as in the end of 'The Morning-watch':

>   O let me climb
> When I lie down! The pious soul by night
> Is like a clouded star, whose beams though said
>   To shed their light
>   Under some cloud
>   Yet are above,
>   And shine, and move
>   Beyond that misty shroud.
>   So in my bed
> That curtained grave, though sleep, like ashes, hide
> My lamp, and life, both shall in thee abide. (lines 23–33)

ANDREW MARVELL

Much of what characterises Marvell's style can be understood by reference to his extensive scholarship and his vocation as tutor to the children of the politically influential. Indeed, both 'The Garden' and 'On a Drop of Dew' have direct counterparts in Latin, written by Marvell himself, which act as interesting commentaries on the drafting process which the English versions went through in reaching their finished form. 'An Horatian Ode upon Cromwell's Return from Ireland' self-consciously imitates the Latin poet Horace's *Odes*, which included poems or songs of formal praise for military heroes and which in turn imitated an earlier Greek form. For elements of expression too, Marvell in this poem draws on the Roman historian Lucan, whose *Pharsalia* presents Julius Caesar in much the way that Marvell chooses to present Oliver Cromwell. Even 'The Nymph complaining for the death of her Fawn' derives from Latin models of mock-heroic verse as a young female innocent laments the death of a pet. 'To his Coy Mistress', despite its apparent immediacy, owes the structure of its argument to the academic discipline of logic, as it progresses according to syllogism, moving between two contrary propositions to reach its conclusion. 'Bermudas', on the other hand, has a quite distinctive style. The run-on or **enjambed, octosyllabic couplets** are perfect for the narrative content and the exotic setting, carrying forward the song of wonder at nature's bounty and thanksgiving to God. Subject and style here combine to give the impression of one of the **metrical** psalms which formed part of Nonconformist worship at this time.

This is not to say, however, that all Marvell's poetry has to offer stylistically is a dry **pastiche** of classical forms and styles; that is not the experience of reading his English poems. There is no forcing in the adoption of classical models, rather the sense of an intelligence so at home with them that they are habitual frameworks for thought. They are vehicles for individual expression which can be distinctive and witty. These lines from 'The Garden': 'Two paradises 'twere in one / To live in paradise alone' (lines 63–4) depend as much on the comedian's timing in delivering the last word as the punchline as they do on the handling of metrical formality. Added to that, in many of the poems the seriousness of the topic under discussion is offset by the creation of a very unstuffy speaker, or **persona**, prepared to make gentle fun at his own expense. Hence in 'To his Coy Mistress', while his loved one searches for rubies by the side of the Ganges, the hapless speaker will complain on the banks of the Humber, a river whose name has **connotative** properties, and even a sound, which make the line teeter on the verge of controlled **bathos**. Equally, amongst all the

allusions to classical myths and Neoplatonic flights of fancy in 'The Garden', the reader is confronted by a near-**burlesque** image of our guide in the place, when he tells us: 'Stumbling on melons, as I pass, / Ensnared with flowers, I fall on grass' (lines 39–40).

These are, of course, essentialist judgements, which can lead to the trap for the naive modern reader of assuming that the way in which a poem is received by us now can offer insight into the individual who wrote it in unknown circumstances many hundred years ago. Literary criticism is not biography, and Andrew Marvell remains inscrutable. But observing the poise of his composition, the care with which individual words are chosen and placed in original combinations, offers safe territory from which to claim for him a distinctive and identifiable poetic voice, albeit one embedded in the culture of its time.

PART FOUR

EXTENDED COMMENTARIES

TEXT 1 A NOCTURNAL UPON ST LUCY'S DAY, BEING THE
SHORTEST DAY (JOHN DONNE)

'Tis the year's midnight, and it is the day's,
Lucy's, who scarce seven hours herself unmasks,
    The sun is spent, and now his flasks
    Send forth light squibs, no constant rays;
        The world's whole sap is sunk: 5
The general balm th'hydroptic earth hath drunk,
Whither, as to the bed's-feet, life is shrunk,
Dead and interred; yet all these seem to laugh,
Compared with me, who am their epitaph.

Study me then, you who shall lovers be   10
At the next world, that is, at the next spring:
    For I am every dead thing,
    In whom love wrought new alchemy,
        For his art did express
A quintessence even from nothingness,   15
From dull privations, and lean emptiness
He ruined me, and I am re-begot
Of absence, darkness, death; things which are not.

All others, from all things, draw all that's good,
Life, soul, form, spirit, whence they being have;   20
    I, by love's limbeck, am the grave
    Of all, that's nothing. Oft a flood
        Have we two wept, and so
Drowned the whole world, us two; oft did we grow
To be two chaoses, when we did show   25
Care to aught else; and often absences
Withdrew our souls, and made us carcases.

But I am by her death (which word wrongs her)
Of the first nothing, the elixir grown;

Were I a man, that I were one,   30
I needs must know; I should prefer,
     If I were any beast,
Some ends, some means; yea plants, yea stones detest,
And love; all, all some properties invest;
If I an ordinary nothing were,   35
As shadow, a light, and body must be here.

But I am none; nor will my sun renew.
You lovers, for whose sake, the lesser sun
     At this time to the Goat is run
     To fetch new lust, and give it you,   40
          Enjoy your summer all;
Since she enjoys her long night's festival,
Let me prepare towards her, and let me call
This hour her vigil, and her eve, since this
Both the year's, and the day's deep midnight is.   45

The poem is called a nocturnal, that is written for the night, but it
could equally be called an **elegy**, not only for the 'she' whom the speaker
mourns but for the speaker himself, who eloquently expresses through a
series of **images** his loss of essence, of being, to the point where he is in a
state of non-being, non-existence beyond nothingness. The poem's
argument rests heavily upon metaphysical concepts of the nature of
creation and humanity's relation to the passing seasons, planetary
influences, other created things and God. The love relationship he
looks back on has a primal, intemperate quality, related to primeval
chaos. Chaos, according to contemporary cosmology, was the only existing
matter before the creation imposed order. That order was often expressed
as a chain of being, a hierarchical structure placing humanity above stones,
plants and animals, but below the angels (see Platonic Philosophy).
The idea of an all-consuming deluge – 'Oft a flood / Have we two wept'
(lines 22–3) – may be associated with the mythic Noah's flood in Genesis
in the Old Testament.

   The shape of the poem mirrors the process of disintegration: it is
apparently a **metrically** regular sequence of five self-contained stanzas
which develop an argument, but it breaks off abruptly and changes
direction on the word 'nothing' (line 22), at the centre point of the fourth

line of the third and middle stanza. The sense of the penultimate stanza can be completed only by reading on into the final one. Editors struggle to punctuate the near incoherence of the **syntax**, which resists containment within the metrical order. Thus the poem's form reflects the antithetical balance between the renewable, orderly nature of creation and the bereaved lover's disintegration into a state of non-existence.

The speaker's affinity with St Lucy's Day derives from its significance as the focal point of the dead of winter. The poet uses **synecdoche** to suggest that the day itself has the properties of a saintly female who shyly takes off her mask of darkness for the seven bare hours of daylight. Celebrated on 13 December, St Lucy's Day was believed to be the shortest day and the winter solstice, when the sun entered Capricorn in the zodiac (the sign of the goat). The name Lucy signifies light; Jesus Christ was described in Latin as *fons lucis*: the 'fount of light' or 'light shining in the darkness'. Many critics have speculated about the identity of the woman whose death inspired such an evocation of devastation as the poem expresses. Lucy Harrington, Countess of Bedford, Donne's patron, who died in 1627, is one candidate; his daughter, named Lucy after her, who died in the same year at the age of nineteen, is another. But 1627 is generally supposed too late for the poem, and it is most frequently considered to have been inspired by the death in 1617 of Ann Donne, the poet's wife.

The first stanza sets up a number of properties associated with the very dead of winter, which the speaker will later allege to be concentrated in himself: a series of diminutions, of drawings in and down, of absences. Related images are connected by verbs expressing this shrinking and dying down. The sun has used up its strength and the only light remaining comes from the stars, thought in contemporary cosmology to derive their light from the sun. The comparison of the stars to powder flashes – 'squibs' (line 4) are sparks from fragments of gunpowder held in flasks – connects the only lights in the poem to warfare and strife. Without the constancy of sunshine, the world has gone into suspended animation, like a winter tree whose sap sinks into the roots. The world is then compared to a person with the disease of dropsy, mad with thirst, life ebbing out until all that is left is in the feet. This is a reversal of the direction through the body that death was generally believed to take, but picks up on the earlier idea of sap sinking so that all of nature is united in what turns out at the end of the stanza to be a **trope**, a **pathetic fallacy** in which all nature is in accord with the condition of the speaker. The downward movement of the stanza inexorably progresses, from dying to death and burial, then the focus changes from the world to the **first person** speaker, who asserts that all that precedes seems delightful compared to his condition; he is the 'epitaph' (line 9) to this shrinking down to death in nature, the final statement, the verse upon the tomb. Unlike many of Donne's openings with exclamations and expletives, this is all expressed in a long **declarative sentence** which situates the point of view and closes down any possibility of contradiction.

In the second stanza the speaker explains why he has this affinity with midwinter: it is because of love. Love is personified as an alchemist. The extended **metaphor** drawn from alchemy also suggests an inversion of normal natural process. Alchemy was the pseudoscience by which some hoped to make gold from base metal. Donne draws here on the same allegations about it that Ben Jonson uses in his satirical comedy *The Alchemist*, suggesting that in the glass jar, the 'limbeck' (line 21), the alchemist seeks to overturn the laws of nature by making a something out of a nothing. Here, it is **ironically** suggested, love, the alchemist, has instead made from something – disappointment and deprivation – a new nothing reborn out of a variety of missing things: the absence of company, darkness (the absence of light) and death (the absence of life). Love has taken the speaker and achieved a new whole, the emotional equivalent of antimatter. Those who would take up love at the conventional time of year, the spring, are warned to take example from the speaker whose misfortune in love has conjured him a new existence constructed out of qualities which are the antithesis of everything vital which love suggests.

The third stanza moves into an explicitly Neoplatonic reading of the situation. The speaker asserts that everyone else draws in vital energy. Here he is referring to the idea that souls descend from the Godhead who is the source of all perfections, in which each soul imperfectly participates. But he alone, in the alchemist's 'limbeck', sucks in everything of worth and makes it worthless. Then the poem moves into its troubling retrospection on the relationship itself. Up to this point Donne seems to be arguing, as he does in 'A Valediction: forbidding Mourning', for example, that two lovers have one mutual soul which makes the rest of the world unimportant, so that when one lover dies, so too does the other. Then the allegation that they as a couple engulfed the world in chaotic and elemental forces moves further, suggesting more pessimistically, as Donne does in 'Farewell to Love' or 'Twickenham Garden', that the whole experience of loving is blighting and self-destructive.

The final two stanzas intensify the imagery of withdrawal, of introversion, of nihilism, as it comes to be applied to the love relationship which, by a **paradox**, is identified with death even as it survives death. The chain of being is invoked in support of the speaker's argument that he is a quintessential nothing. Not only ordinary men, but beasts, plants and stones – all levels of creation – have, he believes, some volition and are capable of love. Even 'an ordinary nothing', like a 'shadow' (lines 35–6), can look forward to renewal when the sun returns. He alone looks forward to no renewing sunshine, for she alone was his sun. The lesser sun, the heavenly planetary body, is in the meantime entering the astrological house of Capricorn, the goat, legendary for lust, and he urges the lovers to follow its lead and prepare for summer's renewal. He alone stays at this temporal and emotional point of absences to celebrate and pay homage to a 'her' who could be either St Lucy or the dead woman, or both, preparing like a priest to stay awake to keep vigil at this the most appropriate point of time.

Negation unites language, form, style and meaning in this poem which modern metaphysics might read as the articulation of a spiritual and emotional black hole. The poem thus tempts the reader to find in it an essential and transcendent expression of loss, but it also remains locked within the integrity of its own particular cultural moment, as its images express many of the period's fascinations with the nature and limits of human existence as it was then understood.

6 **hydroptic** mad with thirst, as in the disease dropsy
16 **privations** deprivations
29 **elixir** potion, concoction
44 **vigil** night watch

TEXT 2 EASTER WINGS (GEORGE HERBERT)

Lord, who createdst man in wealth and store,
Though foolishly he lost the same,
Decaying more and more,
Till he became
Most poore:
With thee
O let me rise
As larks, harmoniously,
And sing this day thy victories:
Then shall the fall further the flight in me.

My tender age in sorrow did beginne:
And still with sicknesses and shame
Thou didst so punish sinne,
That I became
Most thinne.
With thee
Let me combine,
And feel this day thy victorie:
For, if I imp my wing on thine,
Affliction shall advance the flight in me.

'Easter wings' is a **pattern poem**. Writing poems whose external shape on the page presents a visual image relating to the subject of the verse was adopted from the ancient Greeks and was very popular in the Early Modern period. George Puttenham, who wrote *The Arte of English Poesie* in 1589, saw physical arrangement on the page as a legitimate element in poetic composition. The period inherited from the ancient world an interest in the language of emblematic representation in general. The standard nature of classical emblems provided art and theatre with economical and immediately recognisable means of expressing complex ideas, and stage designers for theatrical masques, such as Thomas Carew's *Coelum Britannicum*, drew heavily on Italian emblem books offering an encyclopedic array of visual designs for indicating abstract and moral properties. In this way they could replace the verbal with the visual, whereas in pattern poetry the visual is used to reinforce the verbal. It was not universally popular, however, and one contemporary critic was moved to complain that such poems 'represente the form and figure of an egg, an ape, a winge and sutche ridiculous and madd gugawes and crockchettes' (quoted in Harman, 1982).

There are two competing explanations for why Herbert adopted the affectation of writing pattern poems. Anyone attending carefully to the titles of his poems, for example 'The Collar' or 'The Pulley', is aware of his affinity for **paronomasia**, or **punning**, where multiple meanings are conveyed by a single word. Economy – using minimum words for maximum effect – characterises his poetry in general, and is indeed the subject of 'Jordan (II)'. Herbert also had another poetic project, however, which was to redeploy the forms and conventions of secular love poetry in what, according to 'Jordan (I)', he saw as the single fitting object for poetry – the praise of God. Critics have identified the source of Herbert's devotional pattern poem 'The Altar' in an anonymous verse about unrequited love, written in the shape of a pagan altar and entitled 'An Altare and Sacrifice to Disdaine, for freeing him from love', and have suggested that it provides evidence that part of the project set out in 'Jordan (I)' involved writing deliberate **parodies** of poetry on secular subjects by adopting its forms and conventions.

    'Easter wings', which can usefully be read alongside George Herbert's other poem entitled simply 'Easter', takes the day on which the Resurrection of Christ is celebrated in the Christian calendar as a focus of cautious spiritual optimism. 'Easter' focuses on the pattern of Christ's Crucifixion, death and burial as a movement from fall to resurgence, so that Christ's physical rising provides reason for the speaker's heart to rise. In the pattern poem **images** and **allusions**, all connected with rising and falling, unite to support the poem's central **theme**, which concerns the precarious and fluctuating nature of humankind's confidence in the possibility of spiritual salvation. The poem is presented on the page as the wings of the title. This suggests the wholly optimistic Christian message that Christ's death on the Cross did indeed pay for all humanity's sin, and that his Resurrection was a defeat of death which held the promise that thereafter it was possible for all humankind to join him in heaven and to enjoy spiritual, if not physical, immortality. The wings suggest the wings of angels who are immortal and whose permanent dwelling is heaven, although angels are nowhere mentioned in the poem's text. The poem must be turned sideways to be read and immediately takes on a different shape, presenting a fluctuating pattern of shrinking and swelling which is closer in its emblematic form to its actual argument.

    The top half of each stanza, or the right wing, focuses on humankind's inadequacy. The first recalls the loss of the earthly paradise recounted in Genesis, 'foolishly … lost' (line 2) by Adam's desire for the forbidden fruit of knowledge. The expulsion from Eden is commonly referred to in Christian theology as the Fall, providing a counterpoint to the rising of the Resurrection. The second stanza begins by focusing on the speaker, who has experienced his own fall. He was born, as is everyone according to Christian belief, already weighed down by the sin of Adam – original sin. Like all humanity also, he was unable to avoid committing further sin as he went through life, so was subject to shame and sickness, which he sees as God's punishment. Both stanzas, therefore, present the human predicament through the diminution of the lines until they arrive at two single monosyllables: 'Most poore' (line 5), and 'Most thinne' (line 15). The poverty and thinness are, of course, less physical than spiritual.

The bottom half of each stanza, or the left wing, is the recovery made possible only by the events of that first Easter. Humanity does not contain the means of its own spiritual recuperation; since everyone carries the additional burden of original sin, everyone also requires the agency of Christ to 'rise' (line 7) again and be reunited with God. This is signalled emblematically and identically in both stanzas by a second pair of monosyllables: 'With thee' (lines 6 and 16). In the first stanza the speaker asks to rise like a lark. As well as having wings, in springtime, and so around Easter, larks uniquely sing while at the same time flying vertically off the ground high into the air. The lark's song is here equated with songs of praise sung in church at Easter. The second stanza continues its focus on the speaker's personal spiritual predicament by asking if he may fly towards heaven with the rising Christ. The expression to 'imp' (line 19) is drawn from the traditional sport of falconry. Falcons were kept as hunting birds of prey and trained to kill and retrieve small songbirds, considered a delicacy, for the table. When a falcon lost wing feathers, additional ones were grafted into its wing to improve its power and speed of flight. The speaker, therefore, is expressing again how the agency of the Resurrection improves his chances of reaching heaven.

The poem's resolution is not, however, wholly joyous, but preserves an awareness of the burden of sin, by which humanity is weighed down in this **metaphorical** flight. The final line in each stanza presents a **paradox**. In the first case there is a reference to the Christian doctrine of the 'fortunate fall', whereby Adam's sin was considered necessary in order that Christ could be born and humanity redeemed. In the second stanza the speaker returns to the subject of personal sin and its punishment, celebrating the fact that human suffering in this world carries with it the

The axe's edge did try: 60
Nor called the gods with vulgar spite
To vindicate his helpless right,
    But bowed his comely head
    Down as upon a bed.
That was that memorable hour   65
Which first assured the forced power.
    So when they did design
    The Capitol's first line,
A bleeding head where they begun,
Did fright the architects to run;   70
    And yet in that the State
    Foresaw its happy fate.
And now the Irish are ashamed
To see themselves in one year tamed:
    So much one man can do,   75
    That does both act and know.
They can affirm his praises best,
And have, though overcome, confessed
    How good he is, how just,
    And fit for highest trust: 80
Nor yet grown stiffer with command,
But still in the Republic's hand:
    How fit he is to sway
    That can so well obey.
He to the Commons' feet presents   85
A kingdom, for his first year's rents:
    And, what he may, forbears
    His fame, to make it theirs:
And has his sword and spoils ungirt,
To lay them at the public's skirt.   90
    So when the falcon high
    Falls heavy from the sky,
She, having killed, no more does search
But on the next green bough to perch,
    Where, when he first does lure,   95
    The falconer has her sure.

What may not then our isle presume
While Victory his crest does plume!
    What may not others fear
    If thus he crown each year!   100
A Caesar he, ere long to Gaul,
To Italy a Hannibal,
    And to all states not free
    Shall climacteric be.
The Pict no shelter now shall find   105
Within his parti-coloured mind;
    But from this valour sad
    Shrink underneath the plaid:
Happy if in the tufted brake
The English hunter him mistake,   110
    Nor lay his hounds in near
    The Caledonian deer.
But thou, the Wars' and Fortune's son,
March indefatigably on;
    And for the last effect   115
    Shall keep thy sword erect:
Besides the force it has to fright
The spirits of the shady night,
    The same arts that did gain
    A power, must it maintain.   120

Marvell's poem is situated at a particular political moment. When the Civil Wars were won and Oliver Cromwell declared Lord Protector, the problem remained of how to rule the dominions which he inherited. The Commons in Parliament now had to establish dominion over provinces which were in open rebellion and did not accept the outcome of the wars. There were also divisions amongst Parliament's own ranks. General Fairfax, Marvell's employer by the end of the year in which the poem was written, had delivered military victory but was appalled at the king's execution. On the other hand, militant extremists in Church and state saw the opportunity for a much more radical overhaul of power holding than the centralist rule offered by Cromwell. Ireland was fragmented into numerous factions, not only Royalist and Parliamentarian, but Ulster Protestant, the Catholic confederacy and an array of opportunist tribal chieftains of no established allegiance. Scotland proclaimed Charles II king as soon as news of Charles I's death reached Edinburgh, refusing to recognise the authority of any other power. Meanwhile the Scilly Isles, the Channel Islands and the Isle of Man remained Royalist, and other Royalist military leaders were abroad raising support for retaliatory attack.

Cromwell acted swiftly, decisively and ruthlessly, dealing with one thing at a time. At home he reduced the House of Lords, abolished the monarchy, declared a Commonwealth and free state and incarcerated a number of key radical extremists in the Tower of London. Then he turned his attention to Ireland. Prince Rupert of the Rhine, Charles I's nephew and the Royalists' fearless and charismatic cavalry leader, was planning to bring his fleet there to join with the Marquis of Montrose and an army of Scots supporting Charles II in exile. Cromwell's incisive action caused both to think again, and the atrocities against the Irish people it involved have become legendary.

Critics of Marvell's poem agree to its ambiguity. It was still being censored out of his collected works twenty years after the Restoration of Charles II. It opens with a call to arms, accepting that the young man of substance in such times should abandon scholarship and love in favour of direct military action. As the poem moves towards its description of Cromwell, interpretation becomes difficult. How should we understand 'restless' (line 9)? Does Marvell suggest that Cromwell is unable to settle, to give up war, or that he is what in modern English we would translate as 'tireless', that is 'vigilant'? Certainly the use of 'could not cease' (line 9) suggests a compulsion which anticipates the elemental imagery to follow. He is described in terms of cosmology and science, as lightning, a massively powerful but inscrutable and amoral force of nature, breaking its way through the clouds. There is then an oblique reference to warfare in the following line. Cromwell's first attack is upon his own side, and his driving out of the radical elements with whom he could not work is likened by implication to a charge of gunpowder, which does more damage to that which encloses it than to anything it is pointed towards. The destruction of Royalist country houses and the iconoclasm to which the army had subjected churches are then equated with the destructive force of lightning burning everything in its path until it reaches the monarch. Thus Marvell carefully resists explicit judgement by presenting Cromwell as a morally indifferent force of nature which, like it or not, it is 'madness to resist' (line 25).

There follows, however, a more considered assessment of Cromwell's legacy, picturing him as almost a secular saint, who would have preferred a quiet and withdrawn life. The speaker's admiration of his subject's 'industrious valour' (line 33) reveals that events are being subjected to a value system, one based upon a perceived tenacity and courage which render Cromwell a greater man than the men and institutions that oppose him. The judiciary unsuccessfully pleads the antiquity of the divine right of the king, who is appointed by and therefore only to be removed by God. The pragmatic argument, however, suggests that laws stand or fall depending on the force of their opposition; Cromwell offers the state a different pattern, justified by his courage on the battlefield and the political acumen he demonstrated when Charles I fled first to Hampton Court, then from there to Carisbrooke Castle on the Isle of Wight. Marvell does not, therefore, suggest in this opening section that Cromwell is better than the alternatives in an ethical sense, but that he simply outperforms any opposition foolish enough to stand against him.

Attention then turns to Charles I, who is presented as an actor, 'scaffold' (line 54) being a word that describes any temporary raised platform, erected either for stage plays or for public execution. Charles I by all accounts had faced his own death in an exemplary and dignified manner, rising to his role more effectively than he had managed during his years as monarch. Immediately after he was executed there had been attempts by the Roman Catholic community to have him canonised, and a number of idealised propaganda pictures of him at his execution survive from the immediate aftermath. Marvell's balanced attempt to do justice to both parties rises above the propaganda of the time, but also reflects his own and Fairfax's moderate stance. Certainly he is careful to distance himself and not to approve those by whose immediate action Charles was brought to the scaffold: the regicides are pictured with blood on their hands, literally and by implication **metaphorically**.

'And yet', continues the poem on line 71, the end justified the means. The argument proceeds from this mid point to endorse Cromwell's actions more openly than at first it appeared it would. The quelling of the Irish is presented in an implausibly propagandist form, as the poet suggests that in the end they have been grateful for Cromwell's intervention. This seems inherently unlikely. The brief account of the solution to the Irish problem is, however, simply a transition into a presentation of Cromwell as emblematic of something beyond personal rule. For Cromwell, unlike a monarch, holds power only by the consent of the Commons, which he must, therefore, 'obey' (line 84), so that Ireland is not a personal conquest, but 'rents' (line 86) for the first year's privilege of power. The altruism of Cromwell's motives in conquest is expressed through the **simile** by which he is compared to the falcon, the hunting bird of prey, tamed and trained to give up its prey to the falconer. A number of images then follow which only just avoid suggesting that Cromwell should be crowned: his crown is the plume, which links the falcon to the feathers that formed the crest on the helmet of a suit of ceremonial armour. It is then a verb: Cromwell's actions will 'crown each year' (line 100). The reiteration of the word creates an uneasy ambiguity, at least in raising if not resolving Cromwell's present and likely status in the land. The comparisons then settle down into the purely military, however, as he is compared directly to Julius Caesar and to the Carthaginian hero Hannibal, who resisted the power of Rome. The phrase 'states not free' (line 103) returns the focus of the poem to Ireland and to Scotland, Cromwell's next target, where he will be 'climacteric' (line 104) – where his decisive actions will mark the epoch and prove irreversible. The Scots are described as Picts, the ancient tribe which inhabited the north of Britain, famous for using woad, a blue body paint. It is the minds of the Scots, not their bodies, which are 'parti-coloured' (line 106), however, reflecting in a derogatory way the Scots' practice throughout the Civil Wars of changing sides. Cromwell will hunt out the Scottish Royalists, presented again through hunting imagery as deer hiding fruitlessly on the moors.

The end of the poem returns to the image of Cromwell with which it opened, presenting him again as the tireless warrior, but now demonstrating more explicitly the dilemma which left him no alternative mode of rulership. He is like the heroes of mythology who fight present adversaries by day and the ghosts of dead adversaries by night: the price of achieving power and unity by military force is that military strength must be used unceasingly to maintain it.

The **ode**, a classical poetic form here attributed to the Roman poet Horace, was not yet a very common **genre** in English writing. What it offered Marvell was a form in which he could write an episodic narrative,

TEXT 4 EXTENDED COMMENTARIES
Text 3 continued

but from a particular perspective. Odes were written from within the sequence of events which they recorded, not only to celebrate the exploits of great men but to prophesy what would follow, thereby marking moments of significant intervention in the shaping of history. Marvell is acknowledging that he believes he is living through a time which will change the course of civilisation, and is offering a tribute to Cromwell as the agent of providence in that change.

1 **forward** spirited

4 **numbers** poetry, verses

8 **corslet** armour for the torso

18 **emulous** hopeful, ambitious, imitative

24 **laurels** wreaths made from laurel to crown heroes in ancient Rome

32 **bergamot** a pear tree

83 **sway** rule

89 **ungirt** unharnessed

108 **plaid** woollen cloak, precursor of the kilt

109 **brake** thicket of bracken or bushes

114 **indefatigably** tirelessly

TEXT 4 FRIENDSHIP'S MYSTERY, TO MY DEAREST LUCASIA (KATHERINE PHILIPS)

Come, my Lucasia, since we see
    That Miracles Mens faith do move,
By wonder and by prodigy
    To the dull angry world let's prove
There's a Religion in our Love. 5

For though we were design'd t'agree,
    That Fate no liberty destroyes,
But our Election is as free
    As Angels, who with greedy choice
    Are yet determin'd to their joyes. 10

Our hearts are doubled by the loss,
    Here Mixture is Addition grown;
We both diffuse, and both ingross:
    And we whose minds are so much one,
    Never, yet ever are alone. 15

We court our own Captivity
    Than Thrones more great and innocent:
'Twere banishment to be set free,
    Since we wear fetters whose intent
    Not Bondage is, but Ornament.   20

Divided joyes are tedious found,
    And griefs united easier grow:
We are our selves but by rebound,
    And all our Titles shuffled so,
    Both Princes, and both Subjects too.   25

Our Hearts are mutual Victims laid,
    While they (such power in Friendship lies)
Are Altars, Priests, and Offrings made:
    And each Heart which thus kindly dies,
    Grows deathless by the Sacrifice.   30

Katherine Philips's poems are full of the politics of gender. They draw on male-voice love poetry to construct female-voice poems which are always reproving adjustments of the originals' presentation of the love relationship, and are sometimes outright **parodies**. They also reflect the real politics in which she was embroiled by using **images** of banishment, and **conceits** offering consolation in forced circumstances. She was, as is most notable in this poem, an attentive reader of John Donne's poetry, and her borrowings from him are not merely derivative but are sharply observed critiques.

This poem is one of a number written to 'Lucasia', Philips's code name for her close female friend Anne Owen. Elsewhere she addresses another female friend, identified as Mary Aubrey, as 'Rosanna'. Her code name for herself is 'Orinda'. The adoption of code names is not necessarily devised primarily to conceal the real identities of people; these are classical names appropriate for the idealised lover. Ben Jonson and Thomas Carew wrote love poetry to 'Celia', and Richard Lovelace wrote to 'Lucasta' and 'Althea'. Readers must always exercise caution in assuming that all love poetry is written from the heart to real objects of affection, particularly when the names are so obviously invented and idealised fantasies. In the case of Philips, however, who like most women of the time wrote poems purely for private circulation, the personal nature of the affection expressed is more assured.

The nature of the relationship between Philips and Owen will always be ultimately inscrutable. At a time when women's marriages were arranged by their fathers, and when husbands of any social standing spent long periods of time away from home, female friendship and affection were particularly important in women's lives. Nonetheless, we should be suitably cautious of assuming that the feeling Philips expresses for her friends is sexual. The vocabulary of affection in the Early Modern period, together with the nature of gender relationships and their expression in general, was different from that of twenty-first-century western society, and not only women but men expressed feelings of affection for friends of the same sex in passionate terms.

The first stanza here establishes the relationship between the speaker and Lucasia as something transcendent. The observation of miracles converts people to religion; such is the nature of this love that it should have the same effect on those who observe it. Assertions that love has an elevating and refining power and is, therefore, a type of religious experience are Neoplatonic (see Platonic Philosophy), and the poem bears comparison in that respect with John Donne's 'The Relic' or 'The Canonization'. The following stanzas build up a number of **paradoxes** which describe the experience of separation from the loved one and attempt consolation. The second stanza draws its analogies more narrowly from the doctrines of Puritan worship in which Philips was brought up, particularly Calvinist Protestantism. It explores the paradox that some human beings are elect – preordained to go to heaven – yet this destiny does not get in the way of their free choice, for the elect by their nature instinctively seek out God (see Religion & the Church). They are compared with the angels, who never stop voraciously desiring to be in heaven, although already there. The implication is that the speaker and Lucasia are both destined for each other by a power beyond themselves, but are nevertheless desirous of being together of their own free will.

The third stanza deals with the problem of separation, and draws on Donne's consolatory use of Neoplatonism in 'A Valediction: forbidding Mourning', in particular the **simile** comparing separated lovers to the piece of gold beaten out and extended into a sheet of gold leaf. Philips again employs a paradox to suggest that as the two friends here are separated, their love is both intensified and diffused. Because they are of a single mind, they are indivisible, so cannot according to philosophical logic be alone, and yet they are. In the fourth stanza the paradox is a commonplace in Early Modern love poetry: love is a kind of liberating captivity, and to be freed from it would be an exile; it is more desirable than worldly success and its bonds are its chief decoration. The seventeenth-century Royalist poet Richard Lovelace wrote a song, 'To Althea, From Prison', comparing the condition of being (actually) imprisoned for political principle with that of being imprisoned by love. In both cases he famously concludes that self-determination both in politics and in love mean that

> Stone Walls doe not a Prison make,
> Nor I'ron bars a Cage;
> Mindes innocent and quiet take
> That for an Hermitage[.] (lines 25–8)

Philips's reference to the undesirability of seeking 'Thrones' and her use of **metaphors** of banishment and imprisonment show her participating in the dominant imagery adopted by the circle of defeated Royalists to which she belonged.

The fifth stanza more frankly and bleakly states the pain of enforced separation. Both joy and grief are better shared, and, she suggests, the very identity of each is fixed only by its reflection from the other. She then draws once more on Donne for a further conceit by which she expands this idea, suggesting that it is as pointless being a prince without subjects as it is being a subject without a prince: each defines the other. But here as elsewhere she emphatically, even critically, departs from Donne's 'She'is all states, and all princes, I' ('The Sun Rising', line 21) by asserting the refined mutuality of female love as 'all our Titles shuffled so, / Both Princes, and both Subjects too' (lines 24–5).

In the final stanza Philips returns to the imagery of religion. Here she draws on her developed definition of the difference of female relationships, the strength and enhancement that both experience equally from the sharing and merging of roles in the relationship. The image is of sacrifice, common to pagan religion and to Christian understandings of the Crucifixion. In this sacrifice, however, the hearts of both friends are at once the altar on which the sacrifice is made, the officiating priest and the sacrificial offering itself. Each heart dies 'kindly' (line 29), in both contemporary senses of the word, benignly and according to its inherent nature or 'kind'. The final paradox is the proposition that only by sacrificing themselves to love do they attain the Neoplatonic transcendent and immortal, 'deathless' state (line 30).

3 **prodigy** marvel

13 **diffuse** spread out

13 **ingross** intensify, thicken, condense

19 **fetters** manacles, chains

TEXT 5   THE NIGHT (HENRY VAUGHAN)

Through that pure Virgin-shrine,
That sacred veil drawn o'er thy glorious noon,
That men might look and live, as glow-worms shine,
    And face the moon,
Wise Nicodemus saw such light   5
As made him know his God by night.

Most blest believer he!
Who in that land of darkness and blind eyes
Thy long-expected healing wings could see,
    When thou didst rise,   10
And, what can never more be done,
Did at midnight speak with the Sun!

Oh who will tell me where
He found thee at that dead and silent hour!
What hollowed solitary ground did bear   15
    So rare a flower,
Within whose sacred leaves did lie
The fulness of the Deity?

No mercy-seat of gold,
No dead and dusty cherub, nor carved stone,   20
But his own living works did my Lord hold
    And lodge alone;
Where trees and herbs did watch and peep
And wonder, while the Jews did sleep.

    Dear night! this world's defeat;   25
The stop to busy fools; care's check and curb;
The day of spirits; my soul's calm retreat
      Which none disturb!
Christ's progress, and his prayer time;
The hours to which high Heaven doth chime;   30

    God's silent, searching flight;
When my Lord's head is filled with dew, and all
His locks are wet with the clear drops of night;
      His still, soft call;
His knocking time; the soul's dumb watch,   35
When spirits their fair kindred catch.

    Were all my loud, evil days
Calm and unhaunted as is thy dark tent,
Whose peace but by some angel's wing or voice
      Is seldom rent,   40
Then I in Heaven all the long year
Would keep, and never wander here.

    But living where the sun
Doth all things wake, and where all mix and tire
Themselves and others, I consent and run   45
      To every mire,
And by this world's ill-guiding light,
Err more than I can do by night.

    There is in God (some say)
A deep, but dazzling darkness; as men here   50
Say it is late and dusky, because they
      See not all clear.
Oh for that night! where I in him
Might live invisible and dim.

The idea of using darkness as an source of **apocalyptic imagery** was something Vaughan inherited from George Herbert, who was the greatest single influence on his writing. Unlike Herbert, Vaughan had lived through the Civil Wars and seen extreme Protestant zealots condemn the king as the Antichrist and have him executed. Their justification was that only thus could they fulfil the prophecy of Revelation, the final book of the New Testament, in which, after the Antichrist has been put down by force, the faithful are rewarded with a new heaven and a new earth. Royalist Anglicans in retreat like Vaughan saw the execution of the king and the divisions in the Church after the war as dangerously chaotic, an alienation from God which presaged the end of the world. Throughout his collection of religious poetry, *Silex Scintillans*, which begins with 'Regeneration' and ends with this poem, the speaker is presented as a visionary in the darkness, his recuperation of his own faith a preparation to face the end of the world. The poem interweaves historical biblical reference and individual experience through its dominant fields of **imagery**. The number of words in the poem referring to different states of light and darkness is almost matched by those which refer to sight and blindness. The poem's process is **anagogical**, as it begins by reaching back into biblical history by reference to Nicodemus, the Pharisee in John 3, who came to offer his services to Christ in the middle of the night. The individual speaker then compares his present situation to that of Nicodemus, and uses both Nicodemus's situation and his own to offer bearings on a third, which is the speaker's longed-for union with God on the last day.

The opening stanza of the poem stores up mystery by beginning with a long **inverted sentence** containing two **metaphors** and a **simile** before it arrives at its subject. 'Virgin-shrine' (line 1) denotes the Virgin Mary's body, which contained the sacred body of Jesus in the manner that a shrine holds the remains of a saint, but 'Virgin' also **connotes** purity and holiness in general, and 'shrine' suggests concealment, reserve and sanctity. The 'sacred veil' (line 2) is the flesh, the humanity taken on by God when he came to earth as the man Jesus Christ, and is a reference to Hebrews 10:19–20, more commonly known from its adaptation in the later and popular Christmas hymn 'Hark! the herald angels sing' ('Veiled in flesh the Godhead see'); but veiling is also associated with the concealment of the holiest objects and areas of the church in Judaeo-Christian law and practice.

The second stanza celebrates Nicodemus as one who, unlike the speaker, could seek out and speak to the 'Sun' (line 12) – a **pun** on the 'Son' of God – at dead of night, departing from Nicodemus's common reputation amongst theologians as a man incapable of understanding Christ's preaching. Christ's 'healing wings' (line 9) are taken from the prophecy of

Malachi (4:2) in the Old Testament, and refer to the power of the
Resurrection to heal humanity of the wounds of sin. The connection
between flight, wings and the Resurrection is, of course, central to the
conception of George Herbert's **pattern poem** 'Easter wings'.

The third stanza consolidates the **paradox** of darkness as revelation by
describing Nicodemus's discovery of Christ, who is described as a mystic
flower in a garden setting. The garden is **symbolic** of the primitive neo-
pagan Church before it acquired buildings and set forms; the flower,
together with Christ within it, is surrounded by 'sacred leaves' (line 17), a
pun suggesting the leaves or pages of sacred text through which Christ's
identity is revealed to posterity. This idea is developed in the fourth stanza,
where Nicodemus's privileged situation is elaborated. He did not observe
God as the 'mercy-seat' (line 19), the triumphal image (Exodus 25) of the
Trinity; Nicodemus met Christ in the flesh, a man engaged in a solitary
ministry on earth, resting in a sanctified plot of land and surrounded by his
sleeping disciples. However near to God the speaker can get, he will never
enjoy that experience on this earth.

This is the cue, in the fifth stanza, to shift emphasis to a meditation
of how close to God the speaker can get. It celebrates the night as the time
most auspicious for achieving closeness to God. It has been suggested that
the shift from historical narrative to personal meditation, coupled with the
form that the poem takes on here, defining the night through a series of
epithets in **apposition** to one another, marks the poem's rejection of
biblical narrative as a guide to Christ in favour of the **discourse** of poetry,
and specifically George Herbert's poetry. The technique of this and the
following stanza closely imitates Herbert's 'Prayer (I)'. The speaker suggests
that the night is the time when spirits are released, when the divide
between humanity and divinity is especially thin, when Christ's 'knocking'
(line 35) is most likely to be answered. The quiet 'dark tent' (line 38) of
the night, when communication with God is easiest, is then shattered in
the last two stanzas by the return of daylight and the chaos of separation
from God which signals the coming apocalypse. By now the poem
has established that God is seen with greatest clarity when it is dark;
daylight, the affairs of the world and running 'To every mire' (line 46) – a
preoccupation with material things – all blind humankind to him.

The final stanza returns the speaker to the present and draws its
imagery from the mystic fifth-century Christian writer Dionysius the

Areopagite to create the poem's summative **oxymoron**, God's 'deep, but dazzling darkness' (line 50). In the plain **declarative sentence** that makes up this stanza, beginning with the assertiveness of the impersonal construction 'There is' (line 49), the speaker expresses his desire to annihilate himself, to grow 'invisible and dim' (line 54) in order to be subsumed into union with God's clear night.

The whole poem weaves a tissue of specific biblical references in support of its central **conceit**, which is that spiritual sight, together with proximity to God, is best achieved at night. Darkness is, therefore, positive and pellucid, not obscure, a time to be led to God, as Nicodemus was in the flesh, as the speaker is through religious retreat, and as he hopes to be when the imminent end of this turbulent world comes.

36 **kindred** closely related

40 **rent** torn

PART FIVE

BACKGROUND

IDEAS & DISCOVERIES

The Early Modern period when the metaphysical poets were writing was one of the most exciting in British history. It inherited from continental Europe the major revolution in the field of ideas known as the **Renaissance**, when ancient Greek and Latin philosophical and literary texts were rediscovered. In the same period the Spanish and Portuguese discovered a whole new world, and Copernicus and Galileo moved that world into a new position in the heavens. Small wonder that geographical, scientific, mathematical and metaphysical learning attracted the attention of writers of imaginative texts.

The first scientific thinker to suggest that the earth was not the centre of the universe was Copernicus in his *De revolutionibus orbium coelestium* ('On the Revolutions of the Celestial Spheres') in 1543. Nobody paid much attention to Copernicus until Galileo published his *Sidereus nuncius* ('The Starry Messenger') in 1610, in which he first concluded that Copernicus had been correct, after which the idea of a sun-centred universe gained more general acceptance. The cosmological model that had served the whole of medieval western Christendom (the Ptolemaic universe) was in the process of being set aside, although many writers remained sentimentally attached to it, as the poems studied in this Note show. It was governed not by scientific law but by hierarchies of being. Above the moon the model was of a zodiac, constructed as a sequence of seven crystalline spheres, each containing a heavenly body – Moon, Mercury, Venus, Mars, Sun, Jupiter and Saturn. Outside that was the sphere of the stars, which was fixed and did not move; then an empty sphere, the *primum mobile* or 'first mover', the engine which drove the whole machine; and finally, beyond that, existed heaven and God.

The known world had also recently doubled in size: Spanish, Portuguese and English adventurers had carried on a vigorous programme of exploration, not only to America but also to Japan and the Far East by new sea routes. Their initial explorations led to trade, in slaves among other things, as well as to settlement and intermarriage. Alongside global exploration moved a huge enterprise in map-making, just part of the psychological adjustment to whole new countries. When Europeans had recovered from exclaiming with Miranda in Shakespeare's *The Tempest*, 'O brave new world' (V.1.183), they set about mapping it and colonising it as their own.

RELIGION

Britain was in a state of religious turmoil. Ever since King Henry VIII had fallen out with Pope Clement VII for refusing to grant permission for him to divorce Catherine of Aragon in order to marry Anne Boleyn and had declared himself head of the Church in England, the nature of that Church and its beliefs had been disputed. All the poets studied here reflect in their lives and work contemporary religious controversy (see Religion & the Church).

The central doctrinal ingredient of this Reformation had been Lutheranism. Martin Luther, a German theologian, addressed the central question of what the individual had to do to be saved: his answer was to enter into a personal relationship of trust with Christ. According to his theory of justification by faith alone, forgiveness of sin became a matter between the individual believer and God. Anyone could read in the scriptures the promise of forgiveness in return for contrition: no payment, no intermediary and no institution were required. Later more extreme forms of reformist thought vied with Lutheran humanism. John Calvin, who reformed the Swiss–German Church after 1560, is most prominently associated with the doctrine of predestination and was especially important in the development of reform movements in the English-speaking world, particularly Puritanism. Christ may have died for all, but, according to Calvinism, salvation is only there for those who choose to allow Christ's death to have that effect. They are the elect who have God's covenant and an entitlement to the promised land. Calvinism provoked a deep anxiety in many Christians looking for signs within themselves of election or damnation, and this too is an observable strand in Early Modern English devotional poetry. Roman Catholicism survived as virtually an underground movement in a climate in which religion turned political and no doctrine was prepared to tolerate another.

The metaphysical poets wrote in a period which opened, in 1603, with the union of the crowns of two traditional enemies, England and Scotland. The new king was James VI of Scotland and I of England, who inherited because of Elizabeth I's failure to produce a direct heir. Although the ruling class now accepted the obligation to staff the administration of a growing royal commonwealth, they could not be persuaded to pay for it. James embarked on an unpopular foreign policy and increasingly lived within a confined court circle at a remove from the other forces of Church and state within the country, rarely consulting his disgruntled Parliament. He asserted autocratically the absolute and divine right of the king.

James I had two sons. The elder one, who would have been Henry IX, died, leaving the younger son, Charles I, to inherit the throne in 1625. He was not a successful monarch. In twenty years he provoked a discontented nation to open revolution. While still Prince of Wales he had gone off on an ill-conceived trip to Spain to arrange a marriage for himself, returning after discovering that part of the deal was that he return England and Scotland to the Roman Catholic faith. Ultimately he married Henrietta Maria, a French Roman Catholic. He tried to maintain popularity by ostentatious gift-giving at court, but royal bankruptcy drove him to support this by slapping crippling and arbitrary taxes on his ruling class. Parliament did not agree with Charles's policies, so he stopped calling Parliament, and the result was civil war.

The story of the English Civil Wars, two in quick succession, is complicated. The military campaigns were fragmented and short-lived, but what was demonstrated was that a force could arise from outside the court circle and overturn it. This was not the 'people', if such existed in any meaningful sense at this period, so much as the minor gentry and yeomanry of the shires and the well-to-do merchant class in the cities. The shires had their forces, the most united being the Eastern Association out of which Oliver Cromwell, MP for Hull, formed England's first ever standing professional fighting force, the New Model Army. Events led ultimately to the execution of King Charles in January 1649, and to the formation of a Commonwealth. The Commonwealth, a brave political experiment, became the Protectorate, which Cromwell, as Lord Protector, ran very much like a constitutional monarchy, the problem being that there was no other political theory and no other political models were available. Consequently 1660 saw the Restoration of Charles II, but he was to rule as a constitutional monarch, his power limited by Parliament, because the system of government had changed for ever. The Civil War period was one of colossal damage and trauma to traditional social structures, but also of audacious political, intellectual and religious experiment: that too gave the poetry studied here a particular character.

THE POETS

JOHN DONNE (1572–1631)

John Donne was born in the first half of 1572, the son of a London merchant. On his mother's side he was descended from a number of celebrated writers, including Sir Thomas More, and also inherited their Roman Catholic faith. Both John Donne's maternal uncles were actively involved in Jesuit plots to restore England to Catholicism, and his brother was later to be imprisoned for harbouring a priest.

The young John Donne, however, successfully made his way in secular society, being educated at the Inns of Court in London, in his case at Lincoln's Inn. In his twenties he enjoyed a secure position and affluence in the service of Sir Thomas Egerton, lord keeper of England, and in 1596 and 1597 he engaged in seafaring expeditions, the first a successful looting raid on Cadiz, the second a less successful voyage to the Azores which was initially turned back by storms. By 1601 he was an MP, but in December of the same year he secretly married Ann More, the daughter of Egerton's brother-in-law. He was immediately dismissed from Egerton's service, imprisoned, and had to have recourse to the law to have the legality of his marriage upheld. The next few years were marked by the birth of a number of children and largely unsuccessful attempts to regain social position, while at the same time he was writing **polemically** against Roman Catholicism and resisting urgings to enter the Church. He was finally ordained into the Church of England at St Paul's Cathedral in January 1615 and was shortly thereafter appointed a royal chaplain. The majority of Donne's surviving writings are in fact not poems but sermons, as he preached on numerous occasions before members of the aristocracy and the royal court. Ann Donne died in 1617, having borne him at least eleven children. Four years later he was elected dean of St Paul's and installed in time to preach the

Christmas Day sermon there in 1621. He lived for a further ten years, dying in the same year as his mother and having posed for his own funeral monument (which still survives) wearing his shroud.

His life story is the stuff of legend: the libertine writer of erotic verse who ruined his career by marrying secretly for love; the man born to a family tradition of upholding the discredited Roman Catholic faith who was eventually ordained an Anglican; the priest who became dean of St Paul's Cathedral and the most celebrated preacher of his age. His writings, however, do not neatly compartmentalise according to the apparent phases of his life, and we must exercise extreme caution in reading anything that survives too narrowly as autobiographical. Forty-five manuscripts of Donne's verse survive from his own lifetime, but only one copy of one poem in his own hand, so, like many early poets, it is hard to establish securely exactly what he did write and when, let alone how it may have connected with his personal life. In addition to the sermons, he wrote a large number of love **lyrics**, collected under the title *Songs and Sonnets*, a number of **elegies**, **epigrams**, **verse letters** and **satires**, a long poem called *The Progress of the Soul*, two symbolic meditations upon death, called the *First* and *Second Anniversaries*, and a number of religious verses, including a sequence of **sonnets**. The preoccupations in his writing unsurprisingly reflect what we know of the personal experiences of his life and the culture in which he lived. In the end it is not his illusory progress from erotic versifier to high-ranking divine that is of interest, but the distinctive manner in which in all his poetry the **imagery** of the divine impinges on the erotic and the erotic on the divine.

GEORGE HERBERT (1593–1633)

None of George Herbert's poems was published until after his death. Then, at the poet's request, his friend Nicholas Ferrar published them in a volume called *The Temple*. They are all religious verses, but Herbert, like John Donne, whom he knew, did not find his religious vocation until relatively late in life. The posthumous publication of his poems, and subsequent biographies, turned Herbert into an Anglican proto-saint, and until comparatively recently his poems were studied as examples of perfect piety, compared with the Psalms of David in the Bible, rather than in literary terms at all. The real story of Herbert's life and probable religious views is both more complicated than this suggests and ultimately more unknowable.

He was born in Wales, his parents' fifth son. His father died when he was three, and his well-connected mother, Magdalen, moved the family to London where he attended Westminster School, famous for its music and classical curriculum as well as for the normal grammar school subjects of the age. He was taught there by Lancelot Andrewes, a famous preacher who was one of the translators of the Authorised Version of the Bible, and had what was by all accounts a brilliant career. In 1609 he won one of the school's three places at Trinity College, Cambridge, and embarked upon an academic career which was to last fifteen years. In the same year his mother, a celebrated society beauty, remarried Sir John Danvers, a man half her age. He was also much the same age as George Herbert's eldest brother, Edward, Lord Herbert of Cherbury, who was also a poet and, from 1619 to 1624, the royal ambassador to France. The following New Year George Herbert wrote his mother a letter in which among other things he expresses distaste with modern trends in love poetry and encloses two devotional **sonnets**, demonstrating early signs of the eventual career choice which would mark him out from the rest of his family. At Cambridge he became a fellow, then a reader in rhetoric, and was finally appointed university orator.

In 1624, however, Herbert took six months' leave of absence from Cambridge and never went back, standing instead as MP for Montgomery. Shortly afterwards he became a canon of Lincoln Cathedral, and by 1626 had been installed as deacon of Leighton Bromswold, near the religious community of Little Gidding which had been established by Nicholas Ferrar. During the same period, Herbert married his stepfather's niece, Jane Danvers, and adopted the two daughters of his widowed sister, lately orphaned by her death. In 1630, now a family man, George Herbert was finally ordained a priest and became parson of the tiny parish of Bemerton in Wiltshire. There he lived out the three years left to him as a country parson, lavishing his attention and resources on the fabric of his church, devoting himself to family, parish and God, and writing poetry. He died of tuberculosis.

Herbert's religious position during his years in Cambridge is hard to determine: some of his own prose writings in Latin exhibit High Church leanings, whereas he kept company with many associates who inclined to more radical Calvinist doctrines. Later, Herbert and Ferrar's great project, on which they spent a great deal of their money, was the rebuilding of the Leighton Bromswold church. In Chapter 13 of *A Priest to the Temple* (entitled 'The Parson's Church') Herbert wrote of the country parson's duties in this regard:

> The country parson has a special care of his church, that all things there be decent and befitting his Name by which it is called. Therefore first he takes order that all things be in good repair; as walls plastered, windows glazed, floor paved, seats whole, firm and uniform, especially that the pulpit and the desk and Communion table and font be as they ought for those great duties that are performed in them ... And all this he doth not out of necessity or as putting a holiness in the things, but as desiring to keep the middle way between superstition and slovenliness ...

This shows Herbert's preoccupation with the humble responsibilities of the priest, which was later to find its way into poems such as 'The Church-Floor' and 'The Windows', where church fabric is central to **imagery** and **metaphor**. It also shows an awareness of the type of religious controversy which was coming to a head in England towards the end of his life: 'superstition' refers to the Roman Catholic position retained by High Church supporters, that objects, such as the altar and the font, and the sacraments of mass and baptism with which they were connected, had magical transformational properties; 'slovenliness', on the other hand, may be a jibe at the extremes of Puritanism which saw all trappings of religious worship as irrelevant. Herbert was a priest, who loyally carried out the public duties and rituals of the Church of England, yet his poetry also exhibits the intensity of a personal relationship with God which characterises more radical elements in the Church of his time. Herbert did not live to see the politicisation of religious divide in England which was to feature centrally in the Civil Wars, but he was no more a simple conformist to the Church for which he ministered than he was officially Nonconformist. He died before events would have forced him to choose, and critics will remain divided, therefore, about the cultural position of his intensely intimate poetry.

THOMAS CAREW (1594–1640)

Thomas Carew has conventionally been grouped with Suckling, Herrick and Lovelace under the title 'Cavalier poets'. Derived from the French *cheval*, a horse, a cavalier was an aristocrat trained equally in court manners and the arts of war. The modern colloquial sense of 'cavalier' with its overtones of arrogant carelessness derives from the derogatory use of the word by the supporters of the Parliamentarian opposition in the Civil Wars. Carew was born into the gentry and in his youth travelled Europe serving as secretary to Sir Dudley Carleton and then to Lord Herbert of Cherbury (George Herbert's elder brother), before becoming server to King Charles I and settling into the close circle which surrounded the monarch. Although he went to Cambridge University, he never took up a profession and may have led a dissolute enough life. He became ill in the 1630s, possibly of syphilis, and died in 1640, not living to see the Civil Wars which brought a sudden end to the type of privileged life he had enjoyed.

Most of Carew's poetry was circulated in manuscript form amongst the court circle in his lifetime. When it was first published in the 1640s, it was with a new significance as part of the nostalgia that united the Royalist cause. Charles I's court was characterised by inward-looking pacifism in foreign policy, high personal moral standards and lavish expenditure on entertainment. Carew contributed to the latter by writing a **masque**, *Coelum Britannicum*, which emblematically embodies the values of peace in the state and fidelity in personal relationships championed by Charles I.

Critical convention saw the work of the Cavalier poets, following the work of Ben Jonson, as accessible, stylised, decorous and socially motivated writing somewhat in opposition to the more obscure and radical verse of Donne and the other poets dubbed metaphysical. This is, however, like many groupings of writers into schools and eras, now largely dismissed, and Carew's literary debt to Donne is acknowledged to go further than the formal epitaph which is, nonetheless, probably his best poem. Of the 121 of Carew's poems that remain, thirty per cent or so deal with identifiable events or people. Equally, around fifty per cent of his poems are love **lyrics**, complaints or compliments to ladies real or imagined. Carew's work, however, demonstrates that it is not the subject matter that makes poetry ephemeral, but its treatment. He is certainly a social poet, but he is also a profound and shrewdly self-aware poet, a literary critic who observes precisely in his verse its relationship to the best writing of his immediate precursors and the classical poets on whom they drew. He draws on Ben Jonson and John Donne in particular, not for crude imitation, but reinterpreting their aesthetic for the tastes and opinions of the circle in which he moved. The reader's sense of Carew's penetrating intellectual grasp of poetry as a self-conscious process has led to his being compared with van Dyck, the great painter of cavalier subjects, and rescues him absolutely from any charge of superficiality.

RICHARD CRASHAW (1612/13–49)

Richard Crashaw was a Roman Catholic convert. His father was a Puritan preacher, and his early influences were shaped by the reserve and austerity of the household in which he spent his childhood, but his parents died when he was comparatively young. After a brief time at Charterhouse School in London, Crashaw went to Cambridge University where he met the circle of Anglicans which included George Herbert's friend Nicholas Ferrar. Like Herbert, he stayed at Cambridge after he graduated in 1634, and became a fellow of Peterhouse College, where he led a retired and solitary life, studying Italian and Spanish, which led to his developing increasingly High Church tastes. During the first Civil War, Cambridge was the focal point of some of the extreme Parliamentarian iconoclasm by which church decorations and other evidence of High Church practice were stripped and destroyed, particularly in the uprising of 1643. Crashaw left for the continent, where he could practise his religion without compromise, going first to Leyden in the Low Countries. By 1646 he had converted fully to Roman Catholicism and was found living in poverty in Paris by another exiled English poet, Abraham Cowley. Cowley introduced him to Queen Henrietta Maria, wife of Charles I and herself a French Roman Catholic. With her help he made his way to Rome, where he was employed by Cardinal Palotta, eventually settling at the Santa Casa de Loreto, the sacred place where what was alleged to be the Virgin Mary's house, miraculously transported from the Holy Land by angels, was preserved as a focus of pilgrimage. He died a single man in his mid thirties, only six months after taking up his position at Loreto.

Crashaw's later poetry is distinctive, particularly the collection *Steps to the Temple* (1646), which was later enlarged in 1648 as *Delights of the Muses*.

It is best understood in a European context, however, as its flamboyant use of the metaphysical **conceit** takes on baroque qualities. The extremely austere direction taken by the Protestant Reformation in England, in particular under the influence of Puritanism, prevented the full development of an English baroque beyond the court **masque**; painting and such sculpture as there was moved towards decorative surfaces, maps and emblems, shying away from the visual depiction of emotion, particularly if it resonated with religious fervour or involved images of members of the Holy Family and the saints. Southern European baroque in art followed the Roman Catholic revival, however, which was directed against the growth of Protestantism. Baroque art confirmed the absolute hierarchy of Church and state as well as emphasising the sacramental and mystical in religion. In painting and sculpture the emotionalism and religious rapture of the human subject were foregrounded. Characteristic of the visual arts of the period is Bernini's statue of St Teresa of Avila in St Peter's in Rome, which probably inspired Crashaw's 'Hymn to Saint Teresa'.

ANDREW MARVELL (1621–78)

Andrew Marvell was the son of a clergyman of the same name and his wife Anne Pease. When he was born, his father held the parish of Winestead-in-Holderness, the peninsula north of Hull on the east Yorkshire coast, but moved shortly afterwards to Holy Trinity Church in Hull itself. Marvell was thus educated at Hull Grammar School from where he went to Trinity College, Cambridge. While he was at Cambridge he experimented with writing poetry in Latin and Greek, and had a short-lived flirtation with Roman Catholicism. In 1639 he moved from Cambridge to London, but his father made him return. However, his father was drowned in the Humber while on parish duties in 1641 and Marvell finally left Cambridge for good. For the following five years while the Civil Wars engulfed the British Isles, he travelled in Europe, visiting the Low Countries, France, Italy and Spain.

In 1650 Marvell wrote his poem 'An Horatian Ode upon Cromwell's Return from Ireland'; he also in the same year took up the position as tutor to Mary, daughter of Lord Thomas Fairfax, at Appleton House outside York. Fairfax was general of the New Model Army, the first English standing army, which had secured the victories leading to the formation of the Commonwealth under Oliver Cromwell. Fairfax was not himself an extreme radical, however, and was in opposition to the execution of the king. These views accorded with those of Marvell, who was equally against popish plots and extreme Nonconformist Protestantism, as well as excessive extravagance at court. Nun Appleton inspired a number of poems, including 'The Garden' and the long celebratory poem entitled simply 'Upon Appleton House'. He moved from Fairfax's household to be tutor in Eton to William Dutton, Cromwell's ward and a prospective son-in-law, although Frances Cromwell eventually married someone else. In 1657 Marvell was appointed Latin secretary to the council of state under Oliver Cromwell's son and successor, Richard. Two years later he became MP for Hull, a post he held for twenty years, although he continued to travel widely in Europe. His moderate views and reputedly unassuming, learned and solitary habit allowed him to survive the Restoration of the monarchy unscathed, and to support his more radical friend and associate, John Milton. Throughout his life he wrote prolifically, in Latin as well as in English, and was known to be fluent in a number of European languages. Many of his poems are occasional, that is inspired by public events, but some are more private, witty reflections. He never married, but in his latter years lived with a housekeeper, Mary Palmer.

HENRY VAUGHAN (1621–95)

Henry Vaughan was a twin. He and his brother Thomas were born at Newton-upon-Usk in Breconshire in 1621. They went up to Oxford University together in 1638. Thomas graduated and went into the Church, returning to his native county, but Henry left without a degree and went on to London to qualify in the law, returning to Breconshire as secretary to Judge Lloyd in 1642. That was the year of the outbreak of the first Civil War, which was to cause both careers to take a different turn. Thomas lost his living in 1650 because of his Royalist sympathies, went back to Oxford and took up chemistry, whereas Henry had to give up the law and returned to Newton-upon-Usk to practise as a physician. Henry Vaughan was married twice, first in 1646 to Catherine Wise, who bore him a son and three daughters. When she died, sometime before the mid 1650s, Vaughan married her younger sister, Elizabeth, who bore him another son and three daughters. Henry Vaughan outlived his twin brother, who died in 1666, and he and Elizabeth continued to live in the house in which he had been born until 1689, when they gave it up to Thomas, the son from the first marriage, and moved to a cottage nearby. Henry Vaughan died in 1695.

The story of Vaughan the man is closely overlaid by the story of Vaughan the Royalist Anglican poet, whose way of life and faith were under siege. The major influences on his compositional development were the traumatic conclusion of the Civil Wars with the beheading of the king; the death of younger brother William, aged about twenty, in 1648; his encounter with Katherine Philips; and above all his discovery of George Herbert's poetry. The volumes of poetry for which he is most celebrated are those influenced by Herbert, *Silex Scintillans I* and *II*, written in the last years of the 1640s and early 1650s. These have the intensity of writing which expresses opinions forced underground. The new Puritan ministers had brought in an Act of Propagation in 1650, which sent commissioners far and wide to seek out 'scandalous ministers'. It was particularly opposed in Wales, and especially in Breconshire where Vaughan lived and where the commissioners deprived seven ministers of their livings. It was around this time that Vaughan adopted for himself the title 'Silurist', a name used to describe the ancient Britons. The ancient Britons were driven into Wales by the invading Anglo-Saxons, and took their early Celtic form of Christianity with them. For Royalist Anglicans the Celtic Church came to represent the ideal Church in Britain in a pure and primitive state, as opposed to the present Church which was contaminated by Puritan beliefs. *Silex Scintillans* translates as 'shining rock': in Matthew 16:18 Christ tells Peter that 'upon this rock I will build my church'.

After 1655, although he was to live a further forty years, Henry Vaughan wrote almost nothing beyond a collection of minor poems written for particular occasions, published as *Thalia Rediviva* ('The Comic Muse Revived'). His major early collection of secular verse from the 1640s is called *Olor Iscanus* ('The Swan of Usk'). In the preface to *Silex Scintillans I* he pays tribute to George Herbert's influence in bringing him to the true purpose and form of poetry, which are to worship God, and in it he emphatically retracts all his former verse and hopes no one will read it. In some respects his wish was granted, if not for the reasons he put forward, as it is the verse in the two *Silex* volumes on which commentators concentrate, and from which all the poems studied in this Note are drawn.

KATHERINE PHILIPS (1632–64)

Born Katherine Fowler on New Year's Day 1632, the poet twice changed her name to Philips, first when her widowed mother married Sir Richard Philips in 1646, and then when she herself at the age of sixteen was married to the fifty-nine-year-old unrelated James Philips. She was born in London into a circle of poets and intellectuals: her maternal grandfather was a friend of Andrew Marvell, her grandmother a friend of the poet Francis Quarles, and her stepfather's first wife was an aunt of John Dryden. Her family was Puritan and Parliamentarian in its beliefs and sympathies, so the young Katherine was educated for six years in a school in Hackney. Marriage changed much for her. She moved to Wales, where she was 'discovered' by Henry Vaughan, who wrote in praise of her poems which were already in circulation. Contrary to her family's and her husband's allegiances, Katherine Philips had, like Vaughan, Royalist sympathies, and she wrote poignantly of the Royalist position in defeat in the heavily coded 'On the 3. of September, 1651'. The observable influences of Puritan religion and Royalist politics in her poetry serve as a reminder that the issues and divisions of the Civil Wars were never clear cut.

Philips's love poetry is of interest because not only does she deploy metaphysical **conceits**, drawing much of her inspiration from John Donne, but the subject is subtly adapted to celebrate female friendship and to lament the enforced separation of friends by marriages which took them off to different parts of the country. The female love she describes is more equal and mutual than the heterosexual erotic relationships described by Donne, and on at least one occasion she moves into open **parody** in 'An Answer to another perswading a Lady to Marriage', cuttingly challenging a would-be husband:

> She is a publick Deity,
>   And were't not very odd
> She should depose her self to be
>   A petty Houshold God? (lines 5–8)

In 1660 the monarchy was restored, and John Philips as a Parliamentarian lost all his possessions. His wife was able to protect him because she was so well connected personally in Royalist circles. Her friend Anne Owen, the 'Lucasia' of the poems, married in 1662 and moved to Dublin, and the then widowed Katherine Philips went to live with her. In Dublin her translation of the French dramatist Corneille's *La mort de Pompée* ('The Death of Pompey') was performed to general acclaim in 1663. The following year she died of smallpox while in London attempting, unsuccessfully, to prevent the publication of her poetry. The notebooks in which she wrote her love poems survive in the National Library of Wales in Aberystwyth.

SEVENTEENTH-CENTURY LITERARY CULTURE: THE WIDER PICTURE

DRAMA

Much early seventeenth-century drama focused on current social, political and religious concerns. 'City comedies', such as Ben Jonson's *The Alchemist* and *Bartholomew Fair,* and Thomas Middleton's *A Chaste Maid in Cheapside,* are set firmly in London. Far from idealising the civilised life of the capital which contained the royal court, they satirise the affectations of city dwellers, their material greed, their social climbing through the marriage market, their gullibility in matters of fashion. Jacobean tragedies exploited the new indoor theatres, with plots of intrigue and bloody murder. Frequently these are set in either Spain or Italy, the ideological opposites of Protestant England. Thus the unsettling amorality of Middleton and Rowley's *The Changeling,* for example, in which no single character appears to represent an acceptable value system, is set in Alicante. Middleton's *A Game at Chess* became the original nine days' wonder, running successfully for nine nights at the Globe until the authorities suppressed it. In this play, based on a chess game, the black pieces are thinly disguised Spanish Jesuits, attempting to infiltrate and reconvert to Catholicism the white characters, who are clearly English. In case anyone in the audience missed the point, the Black Knight entered the stage in the Spanish ambassador's litter, 'borrowed' for the occasion.

Set apart from the city was the royal court, which enjoyed the more sycophantic and extravagant fantasy entertainment of the court **masque**, to which Thomas Carew and Ben Jonson were contributing authors. The most important theatrical event of the period, however, was the closure of all theatres by the government of the Commonwealth at the end of the Civil Wars. Theatre was seen as the entertainment of the hated royal court, or of the depraved and libertine young men about town, and fell prey to the Puritan hatred of display and frivolity. Playwrights early detected their common enemy. Jonson satirises Puritan hypocrisy in the character of Tribulation Wholesome in *The Alchemist*, and Shakespeare, probably himself brought up a Roman Catholic, has Malvolio in *Twelfth Night* characterised with venom as 'a kind of Puritan' (II.3.138).

Prose

If it seems that the culture and politics of radical Protestantism were damaging to literary culture in the seventeenth century, a brief exploration of prose writing corrects the impression. The most influential work of the whole period was the translation of the Bible, the Authorised Version of 1611. Written in the plain prose of its time, it has since achieved a, largely specious, 'poetical' status as the most quoted work in the English language. The rhythms and cadences of that Bible, and the accompanying *Book of Common Prayer*, demonstrate the expressive stylistic properties of seventeenth-century prose, which also led to the published sermons of Anglican churchmen John Donne and Lancelot Andrewes (1555–1626) achieving lasting literary status. Their distinctive quality is of unfolding detail which invites the reader to engage in the personal imaginative experience of being present and witnessing the events of the New Testament. The effect was to produce meditative prose such as Andrewes's sermon on Epiphany from which T.S. Eliot borrowed heavily in writing his poem 'The Journey of the Magi'.

The Civil Wars themselves inevitably generated volumes of **polemic** from all parties involved, much of it published in the pamphlets which were the precursors of the modern newspaper. Among all the writers of the Civil Wars, Gerrard Winstanley stands out for his deployment of biblical phraseology and **imagery**, alongside the **rhetorical** structures of successful public speaking, in the making of some very charismatic English prose. He was the leader of the Diggers, or True Levellers, a radical grouping who truly believed that a godly society in which all could hold an equal share in the 'common wealth' could be achieved. His last known work is *The Law of Freedom, in a Platform*, which contains an open letter to Oliver Cromwell, to whom he presents the challenge of a radical God:

> The spirit of the whole creation (who is God) is about the reformation of the world, and he will go forward in his work. For if he would not spare kings who have sat so long at his right hand governing the world, neither will he regard you, unless your ways be found more righteous than the King's ... Some have answered me that promises, oaths and engagements have been made as a motive to draw us to assist in the wars; that privileges of Parliament and liberties of subjects should be preserved, and that all popery and episcopacy and tyranny should be rooted out; and these promises are not performed. Now there is an opportunity to perform them.
> (quoted in Hughes, 1980, pp. 192–3)

POETRY

It is hard to escape the fact that the so-called metaphysical poets' writing lives fell between those of William Shakespeare and Ben Jonson on one hand and John Milton on the other. Shakespeare's 154 **sonnets** have many properties which anticipate the poets studied in this volume. His use of Platonic philosophy and his rejection of the conventions of love poetry which placed the loved one on a pedestal in favour of depicting real and complex sexual relationships are echoed in many of the poems studied in this Note. Ben Jonson, bricklayer and courtier, playwright who satirised city life but wrote sycophantic **masques** for royalty, unsurprisingly encompasses many worlds in his poetry. Much of it was written to attract public attention to himself, some celebrates old values and a great deal expresses disillusion with the worlds of city and royal court in which he moved. It is from Jonson, whose range of poetic subject matter and styles is so eclectic, if from any individual, that his immediate successors learnt to expand the available matter of poetry and to experiment.

There are a number of other contemporaries of the poets treated in this Note whose writings show some of the same impulses and influences. Robert Herrick (1591–1674) was long damned with faint praise as a fine **lyricist** of trivial subject matter. His *Hesperides*, an ambitious collection of 1,130 poems, has lately enjoyed some critical recuperation as an emphatically personalised and generally upbeat record of the encounters and attitudes of a life led through a turbulent period of history, and his poem 'To the Virgins, to Make Much of Time' can usefully be compared with Andrew Marvell's 'To his Coy Mistress'. Sir John Suckling (1609–42) is often, with Carew and others, categorised as a Cavalier poet. He shows evidence of the influence of John Donne's secular verse, but watered down into something more laddish and coarse, with nothing approaching Donne's range or Carew's close reading. Richard Lovelace (1618–57) too earns the Cavalier label. He lived through the Civil Wars and, although he did write a number of lyrics centring on the libertine life of the courtier, his best poetry is found in lyrics which closely observe nature.

Other poets more closely meet the questionable criteria for inclusion amongst the metaphysicals. Amongst them is Abraham Cowley (1618–67), the courtier poet who left Cambridge to join Queen Henrietta Maria's court in exile in Paris. His poetry extends well beyond the range of the court to examine fundamental values, to portray large metaphysical themes through striking **metaphors** and to celebrate its own power. All this is evident in his poem 'The Muse', in which the inspiration for his poetry is characterised as a separate being, which ends:

> Thy Verse does solidate and Chrystallize,
>> Till it a lasting Mirror be;
>> Nay thy Immortal Rhyme
>> Makes this one short Point of Time,
>> To fill up half the Orb of Round Eternity. (lines 68–72)

Edmund Waller (1606–87) and Francis Quarles (1592–1644) have both, with rather less justification, been included in the category in anthologies, although their **imagery** is more conventional in its range. Thomas Traherne (1637–74) has also been considered by some commentators as an Anglican visionary poet whose more optimistic poetry bears some comparison with that of George Herbert and Henry Vaughan. Finally John Milton (1608–74), famous for the epic poem *Paradise Lost*, published in 1667, was also writing throughout the late 1630s and early 1640s, and was a friend and contemporary of Andrew Marvell. Familiar metaphysical themes recur in his earlier work *Lycidas* and some lyric verse.

Katherine Philips is not the only recognised female poet of the period, although unlike male poets they were not published, so the survival of their work in manuscript is largely a matter of chance. Among them Lady Mary Wroth (1586–1651) came from a family of writers and was herself apparently provoked into poetry by an unhappy marriage; Margaret Cavendish, Duchess of Newcastle (1623–73), spent much of her life abroad where she developed an interest in the wide range of intellectual topics which feature in her writing; and Aemilia Lanyer (1569–1645) was an Italian Jewess who came to England in the company of her musician husband who found employment in aristocratic households. Lanyer's long poem *Salve Deus Rex Judaeorum* ('Hail God, King of the Jews'), which seems to have been written to attract patronage, contains some witty early feminist 'explanations' of the causes and effects built into Christian narrative.

PART SIX

CRITICAL HISTORY & BROADER PERSPECTIVES

EARLY CRITICISM

The specific term 'metaphysical poetry' is generally considered to have been coined by Samuel Johnson, the celebrated lexicographer and critic, in 1779 in his *Life of Cowley*. Johnson was drawing on John Dryden's critical assessment of John Donne. Dryden objected to Donne's inappropriate use of metaphysics and philosophy in addressing 'the fair sex' where the 'softnesses of love' would be more apt and entertaining (quoted in Gardner, 1957). Johnson detected the same tendencies in Cowley's poetry. A critical recognition of what is now understood as metaphysical poetry goes back to the poets' contemporaries, however. The revival of the classical **epigram** in the late sixteenth century influenced taste for economical forms of expression in poetry, dense with meaning, what contemporaries admired as 'strong lines'. The poetic fashion for writing **conceits**, the dominant identifying characteristic of a metaphysical poet, was then identified by Ben Jonson, the early seventeenth-century dramatist and poet, when he complained that '**metaphors** far-fetched hinders to be understood' (quoted in Ruthven, 1969). The philosopher Thomas Hobbes (1588–1679) later noted that Aristotle distinguished between good and bad far-fetchedness, and took it to suggest that the more startlingly dissimilar the components in the comparison were, the better.

NEW CRITICISM

New Criticism, the mid twentieth-century modernist critical movement, valued poetry for itself, perceiving in it individual voices expressing essential truths about the human condition transcending the circumstances in which the text was written. New Critics 'rediscovered' seventeenth-century poetry because of its apparent search for what is essential about humanity's relationship with eternity and its characteristic crafting of surprising **images**. The proponents of New Criticism wrote prolifically and persuasively about the poets studied in this Note, and their arguments still offer many useful understandings of the text of individual poems, but their overall assumptions about the nature and status of poetry are no longer treated as received wisdom. It is valuable to read the New Critics on the metaphysical poets, but more valuable to read their work alongside more recent studies which offer fundamentally different principles for the study of the poetry of a past culture. The poet and critic T.S. Eliot was one of the first to admire these poets for the purity and individuality of their poetic 'voices' (Eliot, 1932). Empson (1920) found in their work a justification for his view that a good poem is a rich text containing more layers of meaning than either the poet or a single reader can discern. It was the New Critics who developed the category 'metaphysical poetry', because it foregrounds the formal techniques which the poets of the school have in common. The **conceit** is the instrument of the body of the poem; the vivid personal imagining of a moment is its soul (Gardner, 1957). The poems exist for these critics outside the time of their composition; the fashioning of, for example, Donne's 'The Canonization' is compared to the 'well wrought urn' it describes, a vessel for the perpetual preservation of something quintessential (Brooks, 1949).

HISTORICISM & NEW HISTORICISM

Historical critics suggest that the historical period in which these poets wrote is at least as important in arriving at an understanding of their poetry as close textual analysis. A poem is 'irremediably implicated in its past' (Tuve, 1952), and it is the modern reader's responsibility, therefore, to understand as much as possible about the politics and philosophy of the poet's world. Objective reconstruction of an intelligible context is the desired goal, but one which historicist critics recognise is unattainable. Historicist criticism has given rise to a number of studies of the religious poetry of Herbert and Vaughan in particular (for example Stewart, 1986; Post, 1982), where many critics feel that any understanding of the poems must be limited without a careful study of the religious beliefs, factions and enthusiasms with which the poets engaged. Important historicist debates have included the questioning of Herbert's presumed Anglicanism when Lewalski and others in the late 1970s first found elements of Calvinism in his work (Lewalski, 1979).

New Historicism logically extends the type of debate prompted by waves of revisionist historicist criticism by suggesting that all social and literary identity is something artificially constructed to attempt to impose order, and that understanding can be achieved only by acknowledging the fundamental instability of texts (Healy, 1992). New Historicists refuse to acknowledge the hierarchy of text and historical context. Poems are historical events, consequently Donne's presentation of himself as at times essentially unchanging and at others mutable is an enactment of seventeenth-century Platonism (Aers/Kress in Mousley, 1999). Gender is an important dimension in the New Historicist reading, so that the way in which seventeenth-century love **lyrics** revise conventional gender roles is a political act deriving from English society's acclimatisation to a strong female monarch in Elizabeth I (Guibbory in Mousley, 1999).

CULTURAL MATERIALISM

A major reaction against the admiration of these poets as individual voices in favour of understanding them as products of, and witnesses to, a particular cultural moment has come from the Cultural Materialist critics. Poems do not just appear in the collective consciousness; they are produced in a particular set of cultural circumstances (for example written in prison, written or even commissioned by a particular patron). They are similarly distributed not only by publication, but, as is the case with most women writers of the period, by circulation in manuscript form amongst a closed coterie of friends. Even the most apparently personal poems arise from a political circumstance: the fact that Vaughan was both politically and ecclesiastically out in the cold is not only an identifiable catalyst to his forms of devotional expression, but to the fact that he wrote *Silex Scintillans* at all. Similarly, Crashaw's poetry owes its specific character to its intersection with southern European baroque, the artistic manifestation of the culture in which the poet as exile found sanctuary. The redefinitions of sexuality and the body in the individual works of these poets reflect a wider **discourse** of enclosure and containment, in turn symptomatic of the move from feudalism to capitalism as the organising economic structure. That changing culture was reflected in the enclosure of farmland and in the organisation of the functional and recreational space in the grand country estate. Marvell's 'The Garden', for example, demonstrates a radical shift from early **Renaissance pastoral** poetry (Crewe in Burt and Archer, 1994). The insistence of New Criticism on reading Donne, but equally any poet, as an individual voice means that it fails to acknowledge the part played in the production of this poetry by broader cultural cruces such as the emergence of competing theologies and ideologies, and the redesigning of perceptions of the known universe compelled by the acceptance of Copernican astronomy and by the mapping of the New World (Docherty, 1986). Finally, the emergence of the canon of metaphysical poetry admired by T.S. Eliot and others is the direct product of early anthologising, itself an elite and selective activity (Marotti, 1986).

GENDER STUDIES

Some critics approach the texts of the poetry considered from a point of view which foregrounds the gender of the speaker and of the subject. There were 'particular contemporary limitations of femaleness and maleness' in the period when all the poets considered in this Note were writing, and to ignore these, as much as to ignore politics or religion, leads to a 'blurring of the specificity of the poetry and its concerns' (Hobby in Corns, 1993). In love poetry in particular we are aware of male speakers and female addressees. Donne, for example, does from time to time demonstrate that he can be influenced by the woman he addresses or discusses, but many of his poems focus on the self as man in love at the expense of the other (Estrin in Mousley, 1999). The analytical strategies of the French feminist philosopher Luce Irigaray are employed by Meakin (1998) to generate a reading of Donne's work which foregrounds issues of gender. Female writers from the period have been studied only comparatively recently. The poems of Philips, as well as Anne Bradstreet (*c*.1612–72) and Margaret Cavendish, both mock the cleverness of male writing and reveal the social and economic impotence of women in seventeenth-century English society (Hobby in Corns, 1993).

The apparently introspective and meditative nature of much of the poetry studied here has attracted the attention of psychoanalytic critics. Both love **lyrics** and devotional poetry provide a rich resource for examining how the act of writing a poem can be a particular type of assertion of subjectivity. In Donne's love poems the speaker asserts centrality from the beginning, for example 'For God's sake hold your tongue' ('The Canonization', line 1). Love lyrics are analysed in order to determine whether they present a view of love as something determined by social and political factors, or whether they present the illusion of subjectivity, an attempt to express something more essential than the social identity of the speaker. The language of love poetry is explored as an element in erotic desire, for language defers gratification (Belsey in Mousley, 1999). The act of speaking out is much more ambivalent for Herbert, at once making use of and rejecting the language which asserts the centrality of the subject, thus creating 'collapsing poems' like 'Jordan (I)'. Christianity's principle of self-denial lies behind the impulse in Herbert's poetry to chronicle self-dissolution, by enacting the replacement of the individual creative act by the pre-existing authoritative text of the Bible (Harman, 1982).

Linguistic approaches

A number of critics have looked closely, from a number of theoretical perspectives, at the deliberative ways in which the metaphysical poets use, choose and combine language. It is possible to discern self-conscious structuring principles in the works of all these poets, all educated to a high level during the period of the revival of Greek in the schools and universities, the so-called 'New Learning'. Consequently an examination of their poetry according to classical **rhetorical schemes** and **tropes** reveals a number of controlling principles (Vickers in Mousley, 1999). Herbert's choice of language in which to discuss or address God is an attempt to express himself in the language of Canaan, as opposed to the language of Babel, a divinely sanctioned language removed from the everyday. The ultimate unattainability of a higher form of expression fitting for the subject leads to the suggestion that all he writes is provisional and in some way wanting (Cummings in Wilcox and Todd, 1995). Many of Herbert's titles for his poems are **puns**, or **paronomasia**, based again on a theological understanding of language as God-given. Divinely ordained order dictates a system of echoes and inevitable repetitions that is inevitably an instrument of revelation (Dundas in Wilcox and Todd, 1995). Post-structuralist criticism, by contrast, denies the possibility of arriving at a definitive single reading of any text, because the medium, language, is itself unstable, and each word has a number of possible meanings, depending on the decoding practices of the individual reader (Rajan in Mousley, 1999).

FURTHER READING

EDITIONS

The majority of the poems referred to in this Note have been taken from *A Selection of Metaphysical Poets*, edited by Virginia Graham (Heinemann Poetry Bookshelf, 1996). Other poems mentioned which do not appear in this edition can be found in either *The Penguin Book of Renaissance Verse 1509–1659* or *The New Oxford Book of English Verse*, both listed below.

Elizabeth Story Donno, ed., *Andrew Marvell: The Complete Poems*, Penguin, 1972

Helen Gardner, ed., *The New Oxford Book of English Verse*, Oxford University Press, 1972

David Norbrook and H.R. Woudhuysen, eds, *The Penguin Book of Renaissance Verse 1509–1659*, Penguin, 1992

> A very comprehensive anthology of English poetry from the sixteenth and seventeenth centuries, including examples of poetry by all the authors mentioned in this Note

Alan Rudrum, ed., *Henry Vaughan: The Complete Poems*, Penguin, 1983

A.J. Smith, ed., *John Donne: The Complete English Poems*, Penguin, 1971

John Tobin, ed., *George Herbert: The Complete English Poems*, Penguin, 1991

> Herbert's prose work *A Priest to the Temple* can be found in this edition

CRITICISM

Information on many items on this list will be found in Critical History & Broader Perspectives.

Cleanth Brooks, *The Well Wrought Urn*, Reynal & Hitchcock, 1949
Classic New Criticism approach to Donne

Richard Burt and John Michael Archer, eds, *Enclosure Acts: Sexuality, Property and Culture in Early Modern England*, Cornell University Press, 1994
Essays from a number of different perspectives, broadly within a Cultural Materialist approach

John Carey, *John Donne: Life, Mind and Art*, Faber, 1981

W. Chernaik and Martin Dzelzainis, eds, *Marvell and Liberty*, St Martin's Press, 1999
Collected critical essays – mainly New Historicist and Cultural Materialist

Thomas N. Corns, *The Cambridge Companion to English Poetry: Donne to Marvell*, Cambridge University Press, 1993
Contemporary essays on aspects of the poetry of the period, together with essays on individual poets and groups of poets

Thomas Docherty, *John Donne, Undone*, Methuen, 1986
Cultural Materialist study, repudiating Donne as an individual voice

T.S. Eliot, 'The Metaphysical Poets' in *Selected Essays*, Faber, 1932
Rediscovery of seventeenth-century poetry as examples of 'poetic voice'

William Empson, *Seven Types of Ambiguity*, Chatto & Windus, 1930
Argues the richness of texts as texts beyond the author's intention or the individual reader's understanding

Helen Gardner, ed., *The Metaphysical Poets*, Penguin, 1957
Anthology with introduction setting out the approach of New Criticism

Achsah Guibbory, *The Map of Time: Seventeenth-Century English Literature and Ideas of Pattern in History*, University of Illinois Press, 1986
New Historicist study

Barbara Leah Harman, *Costly Monuments: Representations of the Self in George Herbert's Poetry*, Harvard University Press, 1982

Psychoanalytical study of Herbert's poetic practice and religious belief, including review of earlier criticism of Herbert

Thomas Healy, *New Latitudes: Theory and English Renaissance Literature*, Edward Arnold, 1992

Critical survey of the contribution of recent critical theories to the understanding of sixteenth- and seventeenth-century texts

Dick Higgins, *Pattern Poetry: Guide to an Unknown Literature*, State University of New York Press, 1987

The history of pattern poetry with a chapter on English examples

Barbara K. Lewalski, *Protestant Poetics and the Seventeenth-Century Religious Lyric*, Princeton University Press, 1979

Historicist criticism revising received views about Herbert's beliefs and connecting him with Calvinism

Arthur Marotti, *John Donne: Coterie Poet*, University of Wisconsin Press, 1986

Cultural Materialist study presenting Donne's poetry as a product of its culture

H.L. Meakin, *John Donne's Articulations of the Feminine*, Clarendon Press, 1998

Feminist study

Andrew Mousley, ed., *New Casebooks: John Donne*, Macmillan, 1999

Collection of essays by prominent critics adopting a number of different approaches

George Parfitt, *English Poetry of the Seventeenth Century*, Longman, 1992

George Parfitt, *John Donne: A Literary Life*, St Martin's Press, 1989

Jonathan F.S. Post, *Henry Vaughan: The Unfolding Vision*, Princeton University Press, 1982

Historicist criticism presenting Vaughan's work in relation to his reading of Herbert as well as to the events of the Civil War

A. Rudrum, ed., *Essential Articles for the Study of Henry Vaughan*, Archon Books, 1987

Collected Vaughan criticism

Y

K.K. Ruthven, *The Conceit*, Methuen Critical Idiom Series, 1969
Historical exploration of the metaphysical conceit as a rhetorical device

Stanley Stewart, *George Herbert*, Twayne, 1986
Revisionist historical reading of Herbert's poetry in the context of his life and beliefs

Rosemond Tuve, *A Reading of George Herbert*, University of Chicago Press, 1952
Historical critic

Helen Wilcox and Richard Todd, eds, *George Herbert: Sacred and Profane*, VU University Press, 1995
Collected essays on a number of approaches, including studies of Herbert's language

WIDER BACKGROUND

Thomas Healy and Jonathan Sawday, eds, *Literature and the English Civil War*, Cambridge University Press, 1990

Christopher Hibbert, *Cavaliers and Roundheads*, HarperCollins, 1993

Ann Hughes, ed., *Seventeenth-Century England: A Changing Culture*, Open University Press, 1980
Useful collection of prose texts in modern English spelling

John Kenyon, *The Civil Wars of England*, Weidenfeld & Nicolson, 1988

D.M. Loades, *Politics and the Nation 1450–1660*, Fontana History of England, 1974

Richard Ollard, *This War Without an Enemy: A History of the English Civil Wars*, Hodder & Stoughton, 1976
Accessible historical analysis, with illustrations

Alison Plowden, *Women All on Fire: The Women of the English Civil War*, Sutton Publishing Ltd, 1998

http://www.luminarium.org/sevenlit/
Comprehensive internet site with links to numerous resources on seventeenth-century literature

121

World events	Poets' lives	Literature and the arts
1558 Accession of Elizabeth I		**1558** John Knox, *First Blast of the Trumpet Against the Monstrous Regiment of Women*
		1563 John Foxe's *Book of Martyrs* published
1567 Accession of James VI of Scots		
	1572 John Donne born	
		1576 First public theatre in London
1580 Francis Drake returns from round the world voyage		
1585 First attempted English colonisation of Virginia		
1587 Execution of Mary Queen of Scots		
1588 Spanish Armada defeated		**1588** First Bible in Welsh
		1589 Richard Hakluyt, *Principal Navigations, Voyages, and Discoveries of the English Nation*
		1590 Christopher Marlowe's *Tamburlaine the Great*, Philip Sidney's *Arcadia* and the first three books of Edmund Spenser's *The Faerie Queene* published
		1592 Marlowe, *Doctor Faustus*
	1593 George Herbert born	
	1594 Thomas Carew born	
		1595 William Shakespeare, *Romeo and Juliet;* Sidney's *The Defense of Poesie* published

World events	Poets' lives	Literature and the arts
		1599 The Globe Theatre built; Shakespeare, *As You Like It*
		1600-1 Shakespeare, *Hamlet* and *Twelfth Night*
1603 Accession of James VI of Scots as James I of England		
1604 Union of the Crowns of Scotland and England; peace treaty signed with Spain		
1605 Gunpowder Plot		**1605** Francis Bacon, *The Advancement of Learning;* Ben Jonson, *Volpone;* Shakespeare, *King Lear*
		1606 Shakespeare, *Macbeth*
		1607 Shakespeare, *Coriolanus*
	1609-18 Donne writes *Holy Sonnets*	
		1610 Jonson, *The Alchemist*
		1611 King James Bible; Shakespeare, *The Tempest*
1612 Last burning of heretics in England; Bermudas colonised	**1612** Donne's *First* and *Second Anniversaries* published	
	1612/13 Richard Crashaw born	
		1613 Thomas Middleton, *A Chaste Maid in Cheapside* (published 1630)
		1614 Jonson, *Bartholomew Fair*
		1614 (c) John Webster, *The Duchess of Malfi*

World events	Poets' lives	Literature and the arts
1618 Thirty Years War begins		
1620 Pilgrim Fathers set sail for the New World		
	1621 Andrew Marvell and Henry Vaughan born	**1621** Lady Mary Wroth, *Urania*
		1622 Middleton and William Rowley, *The Changeling* (published 1653)
		1623 Shakespeare's First Folio published
1624 War declared against Spain		**1624** Middleton, *A Game at Chess* (published 1625)
1625 Accession of Charles I		
1627 War against France		
1629 Dissolution of Parliament		**1629** Peter Paul Rubens visits England
1631 Peace with Spain	**1631** Donne dies	
	1632 Katherine Philips (née Fowler) born	**1632** Anthony van Dyck settles in England
	1633 First edition of Donne's *Songs and Sonnets;* Herbert dies; posthumous publication of Herbert's *The Temple*	**1633** William Prynne, *Histriomastix*
	1634 Carew's masque *Coelum Britannicum* performed; Crashaw's first volume of poetry published, *Epigrammata Sacra*	

World events	Poets' lives	Literature and the arts
	1637 Marvell's first verses published	**1637** John Milton, *Lycidas*
1639 First Bishops' War		
1640 Short Parliament; Long Parliament begins; war with Scotland	**1640** Carew dies; his *Poems* published	
1641 Irish rebellion		
1642 Civil War (Battle of Edgehill)		**1642** Closure of theatres
1643 Solemn League and Covenant		
		1644 Milton, *Areopagitica*
1646 End of first Civil War	**1646** Crashaw's *Steps to the Temple* published; Vaughan's first collection, *Poems with the Tenth Satire of Juvenal Englished,* published	
1648 Second Civil War	**1648** Crashaw, *Delights of the Muses*	**1648** Robert Herrick, *Hesperides*
1649 Execution of Charles I; Commonwealth declared	**1649** Crashaw dies	
	1650 Marvell writes 'An Horatian Ode upon Cromwell's Return from Ireland'; Vaughan publishes first volume of *Silex Scintillans*	
	1651 Vaughan's *Olor Iscanus* published	**1651** Thomas Hobbes, *Leviathan*
1652 Act of Settlement (Ireland)	**1652** Crashaw's *Carmen Deo Nostro* published posthumously; *Herbert's Remains* published, which includes *A Priest to the Temple*	**1652** Gerrard Winstanley, *The Law of Freedom, in a Platform*

CHRONOLOGY

World events	Poets' lives	Literature and the arts
1653 Oliver Cromwell Lord Protector		
1655 War with Spain	**1655** Vaughan publishes second volume of *Silex Scintillans*	
1658 Cromwell dies		
1659 Rump Parliament		
1660 Restoration; accession of Charles II		**1660** Samuel Pepys begins his *Diary*
	1663 Philips's translation of Corneille's *La mort de Pompée* staged in Dublin	
	1664 Philips dies; unauthorised publication of her collected poems	
1665 Great Plague of London		
1666 Great Fire of London		
	1667 Philips's collected poems published	**1667** Milton, *Paradise Lost*
	1671 Herbert's *A Priest to the Temple* published separately	
	1678 Marvell dies	
	1681 Marvell's *Miscellaneous Poems* published	
1685 Accession of James II		
1688 Glorious Revolution		
1689 Accession of William III and Mary II		
1694 Mary II dies; William III reigns alone		
	1695 Vaughan dies	

allegory a story or situation with two or more coherent meanings

allusion a passing reference

anagogy the mystical or hidden meaning

aphorism pithy expression of generally accepted truth

apocalyptic referring to the end of the world, cataclysmic

apposition a grammatical parallel

bathos ludicrous descent from the elevated to the ordinary and dull

blazon description of female beauty in the form of a list

burlesque mockery of serious matter by dealing with it in an incongruous manner

cliché boring phrase made tedious by constant repetition

conceit an unexpected comparison between two apparently dissimilar things

connotation secondary meanings and overtones

couplet a pair of rhymed lines

courtly love a stylised, literary convention, representing human love as ennobling

declarative sentence a sentence with a simple indicative structure

dialectic logical disputation; a progress of question and answer moving towards the truth

discourse a piece of writing; a framework of references relating to a specific topic or context

dramatic monologue poem with a single voice which is not the poet's own

elegy a poem of lamentation and loss

enjambed a line of poetry which runs on to the next without pause or punctuation

epigram a short poem with a sharp or witty turn of thought

epithet an adjectival word or phrase defining a special quality or attribute

figure a metaphor which stands for and reveals divine truths

first person told in the first person singular; the 'I' form of verbs

genre a kind or type of literature; prose, poetry, drama and their subdivisions

hyperbole emphasis by exaggeration

iambic pentameter a line of five feet, each made up of one unstressed and one stressed syllable

image, imagery language referring to objects and qualities which evoke a particular emotion or feeling

imperative mood the form of the verb which issues orders

inverted sentence syntax in which the usual subject–verb–object sequence is disrupted

irony saying one thing but meaning something else

juxtaposition setting two contrasting things or ideas next to one another

lyric a short poem, sometimes sung, expressing personal thoughts and feelings

masque courtly dramatic entertainment with emblematic spectacle, song and dance

metaphor a comparison in which one thing is described as being another

metrical with patterned stress and/or accent

metatextual a text that draws attention to its own procedures

octave the first eight lines of a sonnet, or a stanza of eight lines

octosyllabic having eight syllables

ode a lyric poem characterised by intricacy, length and grandeur, glorifying a particular subject

oxymoron contradictory terms brought together in apparently impossible combination

parable a short narrative demonstrating a moral lesson

paradox an apparently self-contradictory statement

parody imitation with the intent of ridicule

paronomasia a play on words; a pun

pastiche a work of art made up of fragments of an original

pastoral a conventional and stylised imaginary literary world of simple rural life

pathetic fallacy the assumed equation between mood and the external world, often the weather.

pattern poem verse written in a stanza form that creates a pattern on the page

persona first person narrator, not assumed to be the author

personification metaphorical language treating things as if they were human beings

polemic disputatious writing, presenting one side of an argument only

pun two widely different meanings drawn out of one word

quatrain a stanza of four lines; four-line units within a sonnet

register the kind of language appropriate to a particular situation

Renaissance 'rebirth', a period of flowering ideas in the arts and ideas

rhetoric the art of persuasive speech or writing

rhetorical question a question asked not for enquiry but for emphasis

satire writing that exposes wickedness or folly by holding it up to ridicule

scheme verbal device, figure of speech

sestet the last six lines of a Petrarchan sonnet

simile a comparison in which one thing is described as being like another

sonnet a lyric of fixed form with fourteen lines of iambic pentameter

sophistry seemingly reasoned but invalid argumentation

symbol something representing something else, often an abstract idea, by analogy or association

synecdoche a figure of speech using part to represent the whole, or vice versa

synonym a word with a meaning identical to that of another word

syncopation the displacement of beats in music or a rhythm so that the strong beats become weak, and vice versa

syntax the arrangement of words in appropriate grammatical form and order

theme the abstract subject of a work

tone the sense of particular manner or mood conveyed by a text

topos a common and recurrent motif in literature

trope a figure of thought, a word or phrase used in a sense not proper or literal to it

typology predictive allegory; Old Testament events prophesying New Testament events

verse letter a poem imitating the form of a private letter

verse paragraph a division in a long poem into irregular syntactic units

Pamela M. King is Professor of English and Associate Dean of Arts, Humanities and Social Sciences at St Martin's College, Lancaster. She is a graduate of the Universities of Edinburgh and York, and taught for several years in London University. She has published widely on aspects of early literature and culture, and has a particular interest in the medieval religious theatre.

York Notes Advanced

Margaret Atwood *Cat's Eye*	Charles Dickens *Hard Times*	John Keats *Selected Poems*
Margaret Atwood *The Handmaid's Tale*	Emily Dickinson *Selected Poems*	Christopher Marlowe *Doctor Faustus*
Jane Austen *Emma*	John Donne *Selected Poems*	Christopher Marlowe *Edward II*
Jane Austen *Mansfield Park*	Carol Ann Duffy *Selected Poems*	Arthur Miller *Death of a Salesman*
Jane Austen *Persuasion*	George Eliot *Middlemarch*	John Milton *Paradise Lost Books I & II*
Jane Austen *Pride and Prejudice*	George Eliot *The Mill on the Floss*	Toni Morrison *Beloved*
Jane Austen *Sense and Sensibility*	T.S. Eliot *Selected Poems*	George Orwell *Nineteen Eighty-Four*
Alan Bennett *Talking Heads*	T.S. Eliot *The Waste Land*	Sylvia Plath *Selected Poems*
William Blake *Songs of Innocence and of Experience*	F. Scott Fitzgerald *The Great Gatsby*	Alexander Pope *Rape of the Lock and other poems*
Charlotte Brontë *Jane Eyre*	E.M. Forster *A Passage to India*	William Shakespeare *Antony and Cleopatra*
Charlotte Brontë *Villette*	Brian Friel *Translations*	William Shakespeare *As You Like It*
Emily Brontë *Wuthering Heights*	Thomas Hardy *Jude the Obscure*	William Shakespeare *Hamlet*
Angela Carter *Nights at the Circus*	Thomas Hardy *The Mayor of Casterbridge*	William Shakespeare *Henry IV Pt I*
Geoffrey Chaucer *The Franklin's Prologue and Tale*	Thomas Hardy *The Return of the Native*	William Shakespeare *King Lear*
Geoffrey Chaucer *The Miller's Prologue and Tale*	Thomas Hardy *Selected Poems*	William Shakespeare *Macbeth*
Geoffrey Chaucer *Prologue to the Canterbury Tales*	Thomas Hardy *Tess of the d'Urbervilles*	William Shakespeare *Measure for Measure*
Geoffrey Chaucer *The Wife of Bath's Prologue and Tale*	Seamus Heaney *Selected Poems from Opened Ground*	William Shakespeare *The Merchant of Venice*
Samuel Taylor Coleridge *Selected Poems*	Nathaniel Hawthorne *The Scarlet Letter*	William Shakespeare *A Midsummer Night's Dream*
Joseph Conrad *Heart of Darkness*	Homer *The Iliad*	William Shakespeare *Much Ado About Nothing*
Daniel Defoe *Moll Flanders*	Homer *The Odyssey*	William Shakespeare *Othello*
Charles Dickens *Bleak House*	Aldous Huxley *Brave New World*	William Shakespeare *Richard II*
Charles Dickens *Great Expectations*	Kazuo Ishiguro *The Remains of the Day*	William Shakespeare *Richard III*
	Ben Jonson *The Alchemist*	William Shakespeare *Romeo and Juliet*
	James Joyce *Dubliners*	William Shakespeare *The Taming of the Shrew*

ADVANCED LEVEL TITLES (CONTINUED)

William Shakespeare
The Tempest

William Shakespeare
Twelfth Night

William Shakespeare
The Winter's Tale

George Bernard Shaw
Saint Joan

Mary Shelley
Frankenstein

Jonathan Swift
Gulliver's Travels and A Modest Proposal

Alfred, Lord Tennyson
Selected Poems

Virgil
The Aeneid

Alice Walker
The Color Purple

Oscar Wilde
The Importance of Being Earnest

Tennessee Williams
A Streetcar Named Desire

Jeanette Winterson
Oranges Are Not the Only Fruit

John Webster
The Duchess of Malfi

Virginia Woolf
To the Lighthouse

W.B. Yeats
Selected Poems

GCSE and equivalent levels

Maya Angelou
I Know Why the Caged Bird Sings

Jane Austen
Pride and Prejudice

Alan Ayckbourn
Absent Friends

Elizabeth Barrett Browning
Selected Poems

Robert Bolt
A Man for All Seasons

Harold Brighouse
Hobson's Choice

Charlotte Brontë
Jane Eyre

Emily Brontë
Wuthering Heights

Shelagh Delaney
A Taste of Honey

Charles Dickens
David Copperfield

Charles Dickens
Great Expectations

Charles Dickens
Hard Times

Charles Dickens
Oliver Twist

Roddy Doyle
Paddy Clarke Ha Ha Ha

George Eliot
Silas Marner

George Eliot
The Mill on the Floss

Anne Frank
The Diary of Anne Frank

William Golding
Lord of the Flies

Oliver Goldsmith
She Stoops To Conquer

Willis Hall
The Long and the Short and the Tall

Thomas Hardy
Far from the Madding Crowd

Thomas Hardy
The Mayor of Casterbridge

Thomas Hardy
Tess of the d'Urbervilles

Thomas Hardy
The Withered Arm and other Wessex Tales

L.P. Hartley
The Go-Between

Seamus Heaney
Selected Poems

Susan Hill
I'm the King of the Castle

Barry Hines
A Kestrel for a Knave

Louise Lawrence
Children of the Dust

Harper Lee
To Kill a Mockingbird

Laurie Lee
Cider with Rosie

Arthur Miller
The Crucible

Arthur Miller
A View from the Bridge

Robert O'Brien
Z for Zachariah

Frank O'Connor
My Oedipus Complex and Other Stories

George Orwell
Animal Farm

J.B. Priestley
An Inspector Calls

J.B. Priestley
When We Are Married

Willy Russell
Educating Rita

Willy Russell
Our Day Out

J.D. Salinger
The Catcher in the Rye

William Shakespeare
Henry IV Part 1

William Shakespeare
Henry V

William Shakespeare
Julius Caesar

William Shakespeare
Macbeth

William Shakespeare
The Merchant of Venice

William Shakespeare
A Midsummer Night's Dream

William Shakespeare
Much Ado About Nothing

William Shakespeare
Romeo and Juliet

William Shakespeare
The Tempest

William Shakespeare
Twelfth Night

George Bernard Shaw
Pygmalion

Mary Shelley
Frankenstein

R.C. Sherriff
Journey's End

Rukshana Smith
Salt on the Snow

John Steinbeck
Of Mice and Men

Robert Louis Stevenson
Dr Jekyll and Mr Hyde

Jonathan Swift
Gulliver's Travels

Robert Swindells
Daz 4 Zoe

Mildred D. Taylor
Roll of Thunder, Hear My Cry

Mark Twain
Huckleberry Finn

James Watson
Talking in Whispers

Edith Wharton
Ethan Frome

William Wordsworth
Selected Poems

A Choice of Poets

Mystery Stories of the Nineteenth Century including The Signalman

Nineteenth Century Short Stories

Poetry of the First World War

Six Women Poets

Notes

NOTES